Bless and Do Not Curse

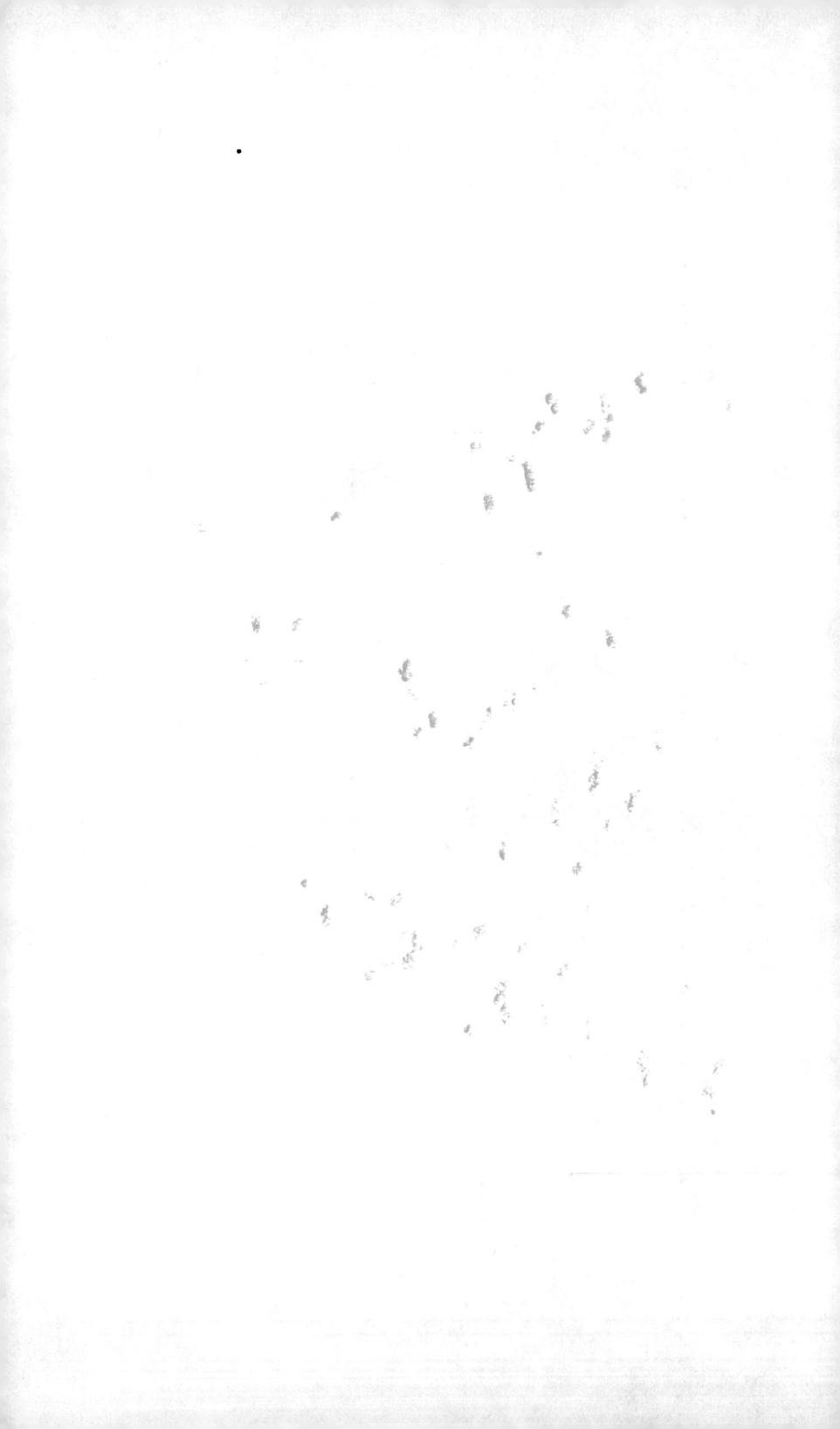

Bless and Do Not Curse

Thomas Aquinas' Moral Theology of Blessings

ISRAEL PEREZ-LOPEZ

PICKWICK *Publications* · Eugene, Oregon

BLESS AND DO NOT CURSE
Thomas Aquinas' Moral Theology of Blessings

Pickwick Publications
An Imprint of Wipf and Stock Publishers
199 W. 8th Ave., Suite 3
Eugene, OR 97401

www.wipfandstock.com

PAPERBACK ISBN: 979-8-3852-2744-0
HARDCOVER ISBN: 979-8-3852-2745-7
EBOOK ISBN: 979-8-3852-2746-4

Cataloguing-in-Publication data:

Names: Perez-Lopez, Israel, author.

Title: Bless and do not curse : Thomas Aquinas' moral theology of blessings / Israel Perez-Lopez.

Description: Eugene, OR : Pickwick Publications, 2024 | Includes bibliographical references.

Identifiers: ISBN 979-8-3852-2744-0 (paperback) | ISBN 979-8-3852-2745-7 (hardcover) | ISBN 979-8-3852-2746-4 (ebook)

Subjects: LCSH: Thomas, Aquinas, Saint, 1225?–1274. | Christian ethics—Catholic authors. | Blessing and cursing in the Bible.

Classification: BV4639 .P47 2024 (paperback) | BV4639 .P47 (ebook)

12/12/24

To all the people who have been instruments of God's blessing for me, especially my parents, Angel and Loli.

Contents

CONTENTS

Acknowledgments

MANY MORE PEOPLE THAN I can list here have contributed to this book in one way or another. Yet, I would like to offer a special word of appreciation to my brother, Fr. Angel Perez-Lopez, with whom I have had the pleasure to discuss in much detail the entire contents of this book. He has helped me greatly with his reassuring insights and critical reading of the original manuscript. To Mary Justice, I am thankful for patiently proofreading the entire book more than once. Of course, despite the assistance of all these people, none of them can be held accountable for the defects of my argument or presentation. They remain entirely my own.

Abbreviations

Catena in Mt.	Thomas Aquinas, *Catena aurea in quatuor Evangelia: Expositio in Matthaeum*
CCC	*Catechism of the Catholic Church*
DA	Pius X, Motu Proprio *Doctoris Angelici*
De Civitate Dei	Augustine, *The City of God*
De Malo	Thomas Aquinas, *On Evil*
De Verit.	Thomas Aquinas, *Quaestiones disputatae de veritate*
De Virtutibus	Thomas Aquinas, *Disputed Questions on Virtue*
De Officiis	Ambrose of Milan, *On the Duties of the Clergy*
FS	Dicastery for the Doctrine of Faith, *Fiducia Supplicans*
GS	Vatican II, *Gaudium et Spes*
In De Anima	Thomas Aquinas, *Commentary on Aristotle's De Anima*
In Ethic.	Thomas Aquinas, *Sententia libri Ethicorum*
In Expositio Peryermeneias	Thomas Aquinas, *Expositio libri Peryermeneias*
In Sent.	Thomas Aquinas, *Scriptum super libros Sententiarum*

ABBREVIATIONS

LE	Paul VI, *Lumen Ecclesiae*
Quodlibet	Thomas Aquinas, *Quodlibet*
SCG	Thomas Aquinas, *Summa Contra Gentiles*
ST	Thomas Aquinas, *Summa Theologiae*
Super Cor.	Thomas Aquinas, *Commentary on the Letters of Saint Paul to the Corinthians*
Super De Trinitate	Thomas Aquinas, *Super Boethium De Trinitate*
Super Eph.	Thomas Aquinas, *Commentary on the Letters of Saint Paul to the Ephesians*
Super Gal.	Thomas Aquinas, *Commentary on the Letter of Saint Paul to the Galatians*
Super Heb.	Thomas Aquinas, *Commentary on the Letter of Saint Paul to the Hebrews*
Super Io.	Thomas Aquinas, *Commentary on the Gospel of John*
Super Iob	Thomas Aquinas, *Expositio super Iob ad litteram*
Super Mat.	Thomas Aquinas, *Commentary on the Gospel of Matthew*
Super Ps.	Thomas Aquinas, *In psalmos Davidis expositio*
Super Rom.	Thomas Aquinas, *Commentary on the Letter of Saint Paul to the Romans*
Super Tim.	Thomas Aquinas, *Commentary on the Letters of Saint Paul to Timothy*

The magisterial texts cited throughout the book are always taken from the website www.vatican.va. I have consulted always the original Latin for the works of Thomas Aquinas. Nonetheless, unless otherwise indicated, I have followed the translations listed in the bibliography. All Scripture quotes are from the New Revised Standard Version Catholic Edition (NRSVCE).

Introduction

SYSTEMATIC MORAL THEOLOGY OF BLESSINGS

"BLESS THOSE WHO PERSECUTE you, bless and do not curse them" (Rom 12:14). This book offers a systematic exposition of Thomas Aquinas' moral theology of blessings, which explains this divine moral precept.

It is not uncommon in Thomistic studies to present a historical analysis, chronologically ordered, of the relevant texts of a given topic. These studies usually pay very close attention to the best available critical editions of Aquinas' texts and to the potential developments within Thomas' thought. This process is very valuable and has been part of the research that has led to this book.

However, for the sake of brevity and clarity, the method chosen for the redaction of this present book is different. Instead of a historical presentation, I have opted for a systematic exposition that presupposes and is enriched by the latter.

I deal here with a *moral* theology. I do not attempt to concentrate on Aquinas' entire theology of blessings. Such a theology is like the material object of this book. But the formal aspect under which this systematic exposition has been made is that of the morality of the deliberate act of blessing another.

I have asked Aquinas a series of questions whose answers have resulted in the book the reader has at hand: What is a blessing? How should we define it? What are the main criteria to determine when a blessing, as a deliberate human act, is morally good or evil? What are the sources of the morality of the acts of blessings? What are the main virtues that lead the minister of the blessings to perform them in a morally upright manner? How should we interpret the divine command to bless even our persecutors and enemies? What are the vices or potential sins to be avoided when imparting blessings?

The organizational principles used to order this book are the four main virtues, which regulate the morality of blessings: veracity, charity, religion, and prudence. There are many advantages to using virtues as the synthetic principle of exposition in moral matters.[1] Thomas notes that this *modus operandi* avoids repetition and provides a clearer presentation.

In the *proemium* to the *Secunda Secundae* of the *Summa Theologiae*, the Angelic Doctor offers the example of the commandment, "Do not commit adultery." If you want to study this moral precept, he says, "you would have to examine adultery, which is a particular sin, and to understand it you must understand the opposite virtue. Therefore, it will be briefer and quicker to treat together the virtue and the gift corresponding to it, along with the opposite vices and the affirmative and negative commandments."[2]

Something quite similar could be said about the morality of blessings. In giving blessings, one should neither lie, lack charity, nor commit blasphemy, sacrilege, simony, or scandal. These sins can only be understood in light of their opposing virtues. Moreover, one needs to understand the divine command to bless even our persecutors.

Hence, it seems that Aquinas would tell us that the best way to organize all that material in a clear and succinct exposition is to concentrate on the virtues involved. Thomas goes as far as saying, in this context, that "all moral matters are reduced to the consideration of the virtues."[3]

1. See Rhonheimer, *Perspective of Morality*. See also Rodríguez Luño, *Ética General*; Rodríguez Luño and Colom, *Chosen in Christ to Be Saints*.

2. *ST* II-II, proem.

3. *ST* II-II, proem.

THE CONTEMPORARY ECCLESIAL CONTEXT

The research that has led to this systematic exposition of the moral theology of blessings was motivated by the recent reactions within the Catholic Church to the declaration concerning the pastoral meaning of blessings, *Fiducia Supplicans* (*FS*). This book is not about the declaration. But obviously, the latter will remain in the background and will make the retrieval of Aquinas on this topic very relevant and contemporary.

FS has been received with both praises and curses by those who have either celebrated or lamented its alleged rupture and discontinuity with the Church's traditional teaching.

Celebrants of the alleged discontinuity quickly alerted the media to lead public and not spontaneous acts of blessings of couples in irregular unions. Thereby, they have violated the very norms laid out by the document, as if *FS* would have made virtuous that which was always sinful, as if the document would be a first step in the direction of changing Catholic sexual morality concerning adultery and homosexuality as actions that are intrinsically evil.

The lack of charity and truth, the scandal, blasphemy, sacrilege, and potential simony involved here have caused and fueled a reaction, which has also adopted an extreme position. Thus, some lamenters of the alleged discontinuity have cursed the document by proposing that it fosters heresy, blasphemy, sacrilege, and scandal. Their position was not only that the celebrants of the discontinuity fell into these sins, they blamed the document itself.

Furthermore, some went so far as to adopt a very doubtful position, contrary to Aquinas, namely, that blessing couples in these irregular unions is something wrong always and everywhere (*semper et pro semper*). In their view, these blessings necessarily mean the approval of sin, because blessing a couple in an irregular union always means blessing and approving their sinful relationship.

Of course, they accept that we can bless sinners but not the sin. But their point goes further. It claims that there is no way that one can separate, in the blessing itself of the couple, the sin and the sinner.

These two groups oppose each other. But they also feed on each other. The more one group laments, the more the other celebrates. At the same time, both groups cause scandal.

It is clear why the celebrants of this alleged discontinuity mentioned above are doing so. But we must also realize that some members of the second group, those who lament that same discontinuity and blame the document itself, are presenting a stumbling block for the weak and uninformed faithful. They are providing an occasion for sin, insofar as their comments on FS constitute a serious difficulty for the weak and uninformed faithful to believe or continue to believe in the apostolicity of the Church and in the authority Christ has given to her magisterium. And to lead someone to deny one article of the faith is to lead them to lose their faith altogether.

AQUINAS AS A HELP TO OVERCOME THE HERMENEUTICS OF SUSPICION

This book has been conceived as an attempt to ask Aquinas for his help and intercession in this current ecclesial situation, to shed some theological clarity and precision on the confusion that surrounds us. I want to offer the Thomistic doctrinal context for an alternative reading of FS, which neither laments nor celebrates such a rupture. I am convinced that Thomas can help us to best understand this magisterial text.[4]

Magisterial documents must be read with a hermeneutics of reform and continuity, or as Karol Wojtyła said, under the principle of integration.[5] The whole of the previous magisterium must

4. Pius X strongly argued in favor of using the principles of Aquinas' thought to better understand the Church's magisterium. See DA. This same idea is clearly affirmed by Paul VI in LE. For a wonderful exposition of these documents, see Andereggen, *Fundamentos de la Filosofía Moral de Santo Tomás de Aquino*, 21–56.

5. See Rhonheimer, "Benedict XVI's 'Hermeneutic of Reform' and Religious Freedom."

be read in the recent one, and vice versa, the recent magisterial teaching must be read in light of the previous one.[6]

While I defend that hermeneutical principle, I strongly contest an alarming intra-ecclesial phenomenon on the rise: a hermeneutics of *suspicion* towards magisterial documents. This attitude of suspicion is not Catholic.[7] It belongs to philosophical and theological modernism, but not to the filial attitude we owe to the magisterium as faithful sons and daughters of the Church, Teacher and Mother.[8]

To oppose this hermeneutics of suspicion leads the faithful theologian into an unsuspecting role in favor of the unity of the Church and against ideological prejudices. He needs to collaborate, through his own theological expertise, in the proper reception of magisterial pronouncements when that reception is problematic or confusing to some.

THE CHALLENGE OF COMPILING AQUINAS' MORAL THEOLOGY OF BLESSINGS

Blessings are the object of a moral precept in the New Law. We find the command to bless in the *Sermon on the Mount* (see Matt 5:44), in Saint Paul's *Letter to the Romans* (see Rom 12:14), and in the *First Letter of Saint Peter* (see 1 Pet 3:9).

Yet, neither the *Summa Theologiae* nor any of Aquinas' major works dedicates a single question or a single article to whether the act of blessing is good, or to whether we should bless this or that. Instead, we find various questions dedicated to maledictions in their different moral species, within the treatise of justice and the proper use of words.

Aquinas' commentary to Rom 12:14 is probably the most articulated exposition of his moral theology of blessings. It offers two important hints for a systematic exposition. First, Aquinas'

6. See Wojtyła, *Sources of Renewal*, 40–41. See also Benedict XVI, "Address to the Members of the Roman Curia," December 22nd, 2005.

7. Perez-Lopez, *Teoría de la conciencia*.

8. See Levering, *Abuse of Conscience*.

implicit moral theology of blessings has a parallel structure to his explicit treatment about maledictions or curses. Second, God's commandment to bless in the New Law is inseparable from the theology of charity.[9]

Yet, serious research into the whole *corpus thomisticum* concerning the morality of blessings bears much fruit. After digesting, as it were, and ordering the insights provided by the Common Doctor, we hope that this systematic exposition of his doctrine opens the door to a reading of *FS* in continuity with traditional teaching.

For the reasons already explained, the best way to organize the material I found are the main virtues with which blessings are engaged: veracity, charity, religion, and prudence. That is the structure of this book, divided into four chapters corresponding to these virtues. The first one will also include a clarification of the very nature of blessings.

The most important Thomistic doctrine I want to underscore in this book concerns the object of Christian blessings. Such an object must be coextensive with the object of charity. In the book, I contend the following thesis: everything and everyone that Christ's heart loves, can and must be blessed under the same formal aspect in light of which this heart loves.

---

9. See *Super Rom.*, c. 12, lect. 3, n. 997; *ST* II–II, q. 76, a. 1, c.

1

Blessings and Veracity

THE GOAL OF THIS first chapter is to establish what Aquinas understands by blessings and to offer a preliminary division within them. After clarifying their nature, we will proceed to offer an opening study of their morality under the light of veracity, both as an acquired and as an infused virtue.

The relationship between blessings and truth is not only with that truth that is accessible to the light of human reason. The morality of blessings is also to be evaluated under the light of faith and the contents of revelation, especially those concerning the moral law as taught by the magisterium of the Church.

NOMINAL DEFINITION AND PRELIMINARY TAXONOMY

To Speak Well

The English term "blessing" comes from the Old English "blēdsian" or "blētsian." Both are based on our current noun "blood." From this viewpoint, to bless has to do with marking or consecrating with blood.

In Greek, to bless is all about speaking well (εὐλογέω).[1] This verb is found in the Septuagint as the usual translation of the Hebrew בָּרַךְ (bārak, "to bless"). It is also present in ancient philosophical and patristic writings.[2] Both the Hebrew and the Greek verbs point to connotations which extend beyond simply speaking well of someone or something. They also indicate the favorable conditions resulting from the declaration of blessing.[3]

The Latin tradition makes the same emphasis with the verb "benedicere" and the English noun for benediction, "benedictio." Once again, this verb and this noun literally point to speaking well, to saying something good about someone or about something.

By contrast, the terms "malediction" or "curse" translate the Latin "maledicere." In parallel to "benediction" and "bendicere," the verb to curse (maledicere) literally means to speak ill, to say something evil about someone or something.

As is known, the imposition of names often provides a direct contact with what is most evident in the human experience of a given phenomenon. For this reason, the Scholastics used to begin their treatises dealing with nominal definitions, thereby acquiring an initial "phenomenological contact" with the reality under scrutiny.

These brief analyses provide a sort of introduction to the nature of blessings. They underscore the importance of the words being said. The act of blessing is all about the "dicere," about the words freely said, and whether those words correspond with the reality signified.[4] For this reason, it is most appropriate to begin a moral theology of blessings under the light of the virtue of veracity.

---

1. Scholars believe that the use of κατευλογέω in Mark 10:16 results simply in an emphasis with the same connotations as εὐλογέω. See Mathews, "Blessing."

2. See Bauer et al., Greek-English Lexicon, 407.

3. Some of the major passages in the Scriptures are Gen 12:2–3; 22:17; Mark 8:7; 11:9; Luke 1:42; Rom 12:14; Gal 3:14; Eph 1:3; Jas 3:10.

4. Even if words can be accompanied by gestures that have an indicative value, those gestures can be traced back and interpreted in light of the words; see ST II–II, q. 110, a. 1, ad 2.

Three Ways of Predicating Well

Commenting on Rom 12:14, Thomas teaches that we can say good or evil about something or someone in three ways: "Here it should be noted that to bless is to say something good. This can happen in three ways: first, by asserting a good, as when one person praises another's good points."[5]

Aquinas continues his commentary by pointing out the second way in which one blesses and by identifying God as its primary author and his ministers as secondary authors: "Second, by commanding: to bless in this way belongs to God by whose command something good comes to creatures, or it belongs to his ministers who invoke the Lord's name upon the people."[6] Lastly, the Angelic Doctor points out that also, "one blesses by desiring."[7]

Since we enunciate something by using the indicative mood, we command by using the imperative mood, and we express a desire by using the subjunctive mood, we must conclude that we can have indicative, imperative, and subjunctive blessings.

Indicative or significative blessings manifest or indicate with words what the speaking person considers as good, including persons and things. A teacher, for instance, can say to his student, "Your performance was good on your exam." This ample use of the term "blessing" as speaking well allows us to identify its basic structure as a natural reality. Those words could be ordered to praise the student or to thank him for his hard work.

We have an indicative malediction, when someone manifests or indicates with words what the speaking person considers to be evil, as when a father tells his son, "What you did is wrong." These words may be directed to a good thing. The father may aim at correcting his son.

---

5. *Super Rom.*, c. 12, lect. 3, n. 997. The same distinction applied to maledictions can be found in *ST* II–II, q. 76, a. 1, c; *Super Rom.*, c. 12, lect. 3, nn. 1000–1001; and *Super Iob*, c. 3, lect. 1, nn. 52–53.

6. *Super Rom.*, c. 12, lect. 3, n. 997.

7. *Super Rom.*, c. 12, lect. 3, n. 997.

Subjunctive or optative blessings do not indicate or manifest the goodness that something or someone has. Rather, they express a desire or a hope of the speaking person who wills a good for someone, for another, or even for himself. They are an expression of benevolence. For example, someone could say: "I wish or hope you have a good vacation."

We can have a subjunctive malediction, when someone expresses malevolence, that is to say, his willing of an evil thing to someone. For instance, one may say to his enemy, "I wish or hope your business fails."

Commenting on Matt 14:19, where Jesus blesses the fish and the loaves of bread before their multiplication, Aquinas teaches that "our blessing is not operative, but significative; but God's blessing is operative, hence the blessing pertains to the multiplication."[8]

In other words, indicative and subjunctive blessings are more proper of spiritual creatures. Imperative or operative blessings, in turn, belong to someone who has authority to bring about the good in question. For this reason, Aquinas already noted that this is the proper way God blesses.

God's Word does what it says: "to bless is to speak good things. Now, God blesses us in one way, and we bless God in another way. For when God blesses us, he makes us good, since for God to speak is to do: 'for he spoke and they were created' (Ps 148:5). But when we bless God, we profess his goodness: 'we bless you from the house of the Lord' (Ps 118:26); 'blessed be everyone who blesses you!' (Gen 27:29)."[9]

The first pages of the Bible present the Lord blessing the universe through his Word. The latter gives being to every creature *ex nihilo*. He blesses all of them so that their natural goodness may grow, multiply, and be communicated. Thus, commenting on the Psalms, Aquinas explains: "The blessing of the Lord always brings an increase in good."[10]

8. *Super Mat.*, c. 14, lect. 2, n. 1247. See also *Super II Cor.*, c. 1, lect. 2, n. 12; *Super Ps. 40*, n. 431; *Super Heb.*, c. 6, lect. 2, n. 299.

9. *Super Io.*, c. 12, lect. 3, n. 1622.

10. *Super Ps. 3*, n. 18. See also *Super Ps. 20*, n. 168; *Super Iob*, c. 1, lect. 2, n. 22; *Super Heb.*, c. 6, lect. 4, n. 315.

Another important example can be found in Christ's words to the adulterous woman. He gave her an imperative blessing when he said, "Go and sin no more" (John 8:11). After original sin, we also find the first imperative maledictions or curses.

Angels and men bless with delegated authority either because they bless in God's name as his ministers, as when the priest forgives sins, or because they hold a position of authority to command the bringing about of the good, as when a father commands his son to be good.

An example of an imperative malediction that parallels the last case would correspond to the judge who orders someone to be incarcerated. In a similar way, keeping in mind that ministers are God's rational instruments, secondary causes, Thomas explains that "God blesses by his authority, but the priest by his ministry."[11]

"AH, YOU WHO CALL EVIL GOOD" (ISA 5:20)

Good in Kind and the Importance of Circumstances

The moral act of giving a blessing is good *ex genere suo*. We do not need a special reason to bless, like a married couple does not need a special reason to have children. In both cases, one should do so until the contrary is proven. Yet, the fact that giving a blessing is a good human act, *ex genere suo*, is not a guarantee that every single act of blessing something or someone is an act of virtue or morally upright.

What one does must be good. But it also must be accompanied by due circumstances and by a good intention. The essence of goodness consists in mode, species, and order.[12]

The famous adagio *bonum ex integra causa* shows that a blessing could turn into a morally evil act for different reasons: "For a

---

11. *Super Heb.*, c. 7, lect. 1, n. 329.

12. See *ST* I, q. 5, a. 5. This is the best light under which one should consider the section dedicated by the *Catechism of the Catholic Church* to the sources of morality. See *CCC*, 1749–61. For a study on the morality of human actions in Aquinas, see Jensen, *Good and Evil Actions*.

blessing, although it is good from its genus [*benedictio autem, etsi sit de genere suo bona*], nevertheless, to be an act of a virtue it is demanded that it should be clothed with due circumstances, that is, that it should be fitting to person and to place and to time."[13]

Among those due circumstances, the veracity of a blessing constitutes an important element of its basic morality. It is not the only element to be considered. But it is one of the most basic. The goods declared as such by the blessing must be truly so. Otherwise, the words of Isaiah will condemn us: "Ah, you who call evil good" (Isa 5:20).

Truthful Commands and Wishes?

The human person is capable of verbal communication because he is naturally called to the *communio personarum* of life in society. To say the truth is a matter of justice.

In the *Summa Theologiae*, in his treatment of the virtue of veracity, Aquinas explains this same doctrine, appealing to an important principle concerning the debt in-built in our social nature: "Since man is a social animal, one man naturally owes another whatever is necessary for the preservation of human society."[14]

Based on this principle, the Angelic Doctor points out that "it would be impossible for men to live together, unless they believed one another, as declaring the truth one to another."[15] This is how veracity is a matter of justice. In a way, it deals with something being due.

The veracity of indicative blessings rests upon the fact that internal words are naturally ordered to the knowledge of the truth, while external words, like the ones used in the blessing, are naturally ordered to the communication of said truth through enunciations.

---

13. *Quodlibet* IV, q. 12, a. 1, ad 13.
14. *ST* II–II, q. 109, a. 3, ad 1.
15. *ST* II–II, q. 109, a. 3, ad 1.

External words are ordered by nature to manifest what one really thinks, to communicate his own internal words. Thus, commenting on Aristotle, Aquinas says that "enunciation is speech in which there is truth or falsity."[16]

Our preliminary taxonomy of blessings, however, has identified not only indicative blessings, but also two more: imperative and subjunctive. What about the expression of desires and commands? How is truth present in them? Thomas argues that none of those two are subject to truth or falsity.

To comprehend this affirmation, we need to look at Aquinas' commentary on Aristotle's *Peryermenias*. Therein, the Angelic Doctor explains that our intellect not only conceives the truth of a thing, but it also "belongs to its office to direct and order others in accordance with what it conceives."[17]

Hence, we have alternative forms of speech other than the one that signifies the concept of the mind, namely, enunciative speech. We also have "other kinds of speech to signify the order of reason by which others are directed."[18]

It is within this context that we encounter commands and desires in the forms of imperative and deprecative forms of speech: "imperative speech is used with regard to inferiors, deprecative with regard to superiors."[19]

Thomas is crystal clear. Truth does not belong to imperatives and deprecations: "truth or falsity is not found in any of them, but only in enunciative speech, which signifies what the mind conceives from things."[20]

Should we then conclude that there is no such thing as the truth of an imperative or subjunctive blessing? No. Rather, we

16. *In I Expositio Peryermeneias*, lect. 7, n. 83. The connections of mental words with truth and of external words with veracity manifest that all intellectual creatures are made for the last end of the universe, namely, Truth. This is the most precious common good toward which all human conversation is oriented. See *SCG* I, 1.

17. *In I Expositio Peryermeneias*, lect. 1, n. 86.

18. *In I Expositio Peryermeneias*, lect. 1, n. 86.

19. *In I Expositio Peryermeneias*, lect. 1, n. 86.

20. *In I Expositio Peryermeneias*, lect. 1, n. 86.

need to make an important distinction between being the subject of truth in a direct manner and being so in a mediated way.

A Deeper Look at the Act of Command

A deeper analysis of the texts of Aquinas, within the whole context of his moral theory of action, shows that desires and commands are subjects of truth in a *mediated* way. The command to "clean the kitchen" is neither true nor false. Yet, such a command presupposes in the commanding person a previous act of the will, in turn informed by an indicative judgment concerning the goodness of cleaning the kitchen. And this last judgment is the subject of truth. Let us explain with more detail our position here.

Carefully consider the following text from the *Prima Secundae* on the nature of command, and pay close attention to the way in which Thomas describes how the acts of the intellect and the will bear on one another:

> Command is an act of the reason *presupposing*, however, *an act of the will*. In proof of this, we must take note that, since *the acts of the reason and of the will can be brought to bear on one another*, insofar as the reason reasons about willing, and the will wills to reason, the result is that the act of the reason precedes the act of the will, and conversely. And since *the power of the preceding act continues in the act that follows*, it happens sometimes that there is an act of the will insofar as *it retains in itself something of an act of the reason*, as we have stated in reference to use and choice; and conversely, that there is an act of the reason insofar as *it retains in itself something of an act of the will*.[21]

When Thomas says that the acts of the intellect and the will can be brought to bear on one another, thereby retaining in one what comes from the other, he is thinking about a whole set of pairs of acts (six pairs in total) that vertebrate his understanding of human action.[22]

21. See *ST* I–II, q. 17, a. 1, c; emphasis added.
22. See Brock, *Action and Conduct*.

The following chart summarizes Aquinas' synthetic presentation in the *Prima Secundae* and a long tradition of commentators. The chart does not follow the order of the *Summa*, in which Aquinas presents them from the viewpoint of the fruition of the end and the order of execution. Rather, the chart we are about to introduce offers a complementary genetic presentation of human action from the order of intention to the order of execution.

Nevertheless, this chart may be helpful for the person who is not an expert in Thomas' theory of action to identify those acts of the intellect and the will which can be brought to bear on one another.

The Intellect and the Will in the Process of Human Action

Consider the following table taken from the monographic study of Daniel Westberg.[23]

Process of Human Action	
Intellect	Will
About the end	
1. Apprehension of the end (*apprehensio; simplex intellectus*)	2. Wish; willing the end (*velle; simplex voluntas*)
3. Judgment about the end (*judicium circa finem* or *iudicium synderesis*)	4. Intention (*intentio*)
About the means	
5. Counsel (*consilium*)	6. Consent (*Consensus*)
7. Practical judgment (*iudicium practicum*)	8. Choice (*electio*)
Execution	
9. Command (*imperium*)	10. Use; application (*usus; usus activus*)
11. Judgment of the end attained	12. Enjoyment; completion (*fruitio*)

Let us use an example that illustrates this process. I will take advantage of this example to also point out how the virtue of

23. See Westberg, *Right Practical Reason*.

prudence perfects practical reason. This point will become useful in our fourth chapter.

We all apprehend with our minds that health is a good we need to be happy. The apprehension of health as a good is attained through simple apprehension or *simplex intellectus*. It is a form of understanding that needs no discursive reasoning process. One does not need a syllogism to comprehend that it is good to be healthy.

Correspondingly to this simple understanding or apprehension is the wish or the simple volition we have toward this good. We wish to be healthy. Sometimes Aquinas refers to this simple volition as *voluntas ut natura*, contrasting it with the volition of something through the deliberation of reason, *voluntas ut ratio*.

> The act of the will, inasmuch as it is drawn to anything desired of itself, as health, which act is called by Damascene *thelesis*—i.e., simple will, and by the masters will as nature, is different from the act of the will as it is drawn to anything that is desired only in order to something else, as to take medicine; and this act of the will Damascene calls *boulesis*—i.e., counseling will, and the masters, will as reason.[24]

This wish or simple volition, however, is informed by the act of understanding that we explained. The act of understanding is within the act of simple volition or wish. It is really present in the will.

However, one thing is to have a wish to be healthy and quite another is to form an intention in the will to be healthy. For the latter to take place, one needs to judge health as an end or goal of the will. Such judgment leads to the forming of the intention in the will.

Note well that the judgment made about health as an end or goal is also influenced by the simple volition that preceded it. There is a bearing of the previous act of the will on the act of the intellect that composes and divides about health as an end.

The birth of that intention leads the intellect to enter the realm of prudence, namely, the realm of the things that are conducive to the end (*ea quae sunt ad finem*), the realm of what

24. *ST* III, q. 18, a. 3, c.

we colloquially refer to as the means to attain the intended goal. This realm contains two important intellectual acts: counsel and judgment.

The intellect inquires as to the different means to improve one's health. Once again, the inquiry bears the impetus of the preceding act of the will, namely, the act of intention. The different options considered as good are approved by the volitional act of consent.

The act of counsel informs the act of consent, and the act of consent fuels or motivates the intellect for the next step: the intellect needs to judge which one of the approved options will inform the choice of the will, which option is the best in the current circumstances, given what is possible.

The will does not choose something without a reason. There is always a judgment informing our choices. This judgment is called the last judgment of the process of deliberation. And it is the will, in the moment of choice, that makes this last judgment to be last.

After the choice has been made, we have the intellectual act perfected by the virtue of prudence that interests us most: command. The act of command inaugurates the process of human action which we call execution. Just as it happened in the other cases, the act of command is motivated by the preceding act of the will, namely, choice. In turn, that choice was informed by an act of the intellect, a judgment.

The act of command informs the use of the will of other faculties for the execution of the action, for instance to go to the gym. When the action is completed, the intellect judges that the goal has been attained. Correspondingly, the will experiences the joy or fruition characteristic of having achieved an intended goal.

Subject of Truth in a Mediated Way

After our brief presentation on the synergy between intellect and will in the process of human action, the main point we must concentrate on and come back to is the last judgment of reason which informs choice.

That judgment is an enunciation. It informs the choice, and that choice is the act of the will presupposed in command. For this reason, we can argue for a mediated way in which truth is present in commands.

In this manner, every command and desire can be traced back to enunciations. Thus, we can affirm that imperative and subjunctive blessings are not the subject of truth in a direct manner. Yet, they are so indirectly or in a mediated way, insofar as they contain within themselves an enunciation in the judgment of choice.[25]

Therefore, by treating of the veracity of indicative blessings, we will touch upon all the essential elements of the veracity of subjunctive and imperative blessings.

Every indicative judgment is a pronouncement of the mind. It is the second operation of the intellect whereby we compose or divide, affirm or deny something. A judgment affirms something about the object being judged. But it also affirms the truth of that very judgment. It also asserts its conformity with reality (*adequatio rei et intellectus*).

Mental words, in which the human mind expresses the knowledge it has of real things, are naturally connected with truth as the good of the intellect. The privation of this due good is an evil.

When the intellect is viewed apart from its connection with the will, such an evil is merely natural. It is sheer ignorance or error. It is not a moral evil. For ignorance and error to be a moral evil, one must consider the role of the will, which can and must move the intellect to know certain things.[26]

For instance, ordained ministers have the duty of sufficiently knowing sacred doctrine to judge which things could be blessed because they are truly good. They can attain that knowledge, and they are expected to have it. Ignorance or error in this terrain, through the lack of diligence in their own studies and formation, is the effect of a privation of a due good of the intellect, which results from free actions or omissions, and that is imputable.

25. See Millán-Puelles, *Libre Afirmación*.
26. See Millán-Puelles, *Interés*.

The Unity of the Interior and Exterior Act

The manifestation or falsification of what is hidden in the human heart of the speaking person is a voluntary act, with which the will moves the intellect and the body to express itself with words and gestures. To say something is not an elicited act of the will. It is an elicited act of the intellect commanded from the viewpoint of the will.

To comprehend the unity of the commanding or interior act of the will, on the one hand, and the commanded act of the intellect as the exterior act of the will, on the other hand, is decisive to judge the morality of every blessing as an instance of saying something. Pay close attention to the following key text from Aquinas:

> A moral act takes its species from two things, its *object*, and its *end*: for the end is the object of the will, which is the first mover in moral acts. And the power moved by the will has its own object, which is the proximate object of the voluntary act, and stands in relation to the will's act towards the end, as material to formal.[27]

The proximate object of the blessing as a voluntary act are the words that manifest the good. The power of the soul that has those words as its object is the intellect. The latter is moved in the voluntary act by the will. The object of the will is the end that moves it.

To will such an end behaves like a form. Following Aristotle, Aquinas teaches that form is act (*forma est actus*).[28] Thus, if we follow Thomas' analogy, to will such an end is *like* an act, with respect to the matter or potency that is the proximate object, namely, the saying of the words above mentioned.

But form also gives the species (*forma dat speciem*).[29] A natural substance is what it is, thanks to its form.[30] A cat or a dog are that kind of animal precisely because of their substantial form, their soul. Again, following the analogy between natural

---

27. *ST* II–II, q. 110, a. 1, c; emphasis added.

28. See, for example, *In II De Anima*, lect. 4, n. 275.

29. See *De Virtutibus*, q. 5, a. 3, c; *De Malo*, q. 9, a. 2, arg. 10.

30. See Brock, *Philosophy of Saint Thomas Aquinas*.

substances and human actions, we must conclude that the exterior act of uttering words is specified or actualized by the interior act of the will with respect to the end.

Consider the example of a blessing in which the minister lies. Its essence consists in *deliberately* saying something false. To say something false is not yet a formal lie. One must do so deliberately, knowing that he is speaking *contra mentem*, that what he is saying is not what he knows or thinks.

As Thomas teaches, lying is something bad *ex genere suo*, because it bears on what he calls "undue matter." Indeed, "words are naturally signs of intellectual acts, it is unnatural and undue for anyone to signify by words something that is not in his mind."[31]

To do so with the intent of deceiving is a proper effect present in a more "perfect" lie. But we need to remember that "the desire to deceive belongs to the perfection of lying, but not to its species."[32]

The minister who gives a blessing calling good what in reality is evil, being aware of that discrepancy and deliberately willing to speak against his mind, is already lying even if he does not yet intend to deceive the person being blessed. That being aware of the discrepancy and deliberately willing to speak against one's mind is the end of the will mentioned by Aquinas. That end informs, as its matter, the words that are the object of the intellect. Since form is act and gives the species, willing this end specifies the exterior act of uttering words. It gives to those words the moral species of lying.[33]

A Real Definition of Blessings

Aquinas does not offer an explicit real definition of a blessing. But he provides one for curses. The latter can be used to infer the former: "If a man commands or desires another's evil, as evil, being intent on the evil itself, then evil speaking will be unlawful in both

---

31. *ST* II–II, q. 110, a. 3, c.
32. *ST* II–II, q. 110, a. 1, ad 3.
33. See *Super Eph.*, c. 1, lect. 1, n. 7.

ways, and this is what is meant by cursing [*et hoc est maledicere per se loquendo*]."[34]

Mutatis mutandis, the moral act of blessing must consist in deliberately saying, commanding, or desiring the good under the aspect of goodness to foster the good. This fostering must be viewed as a sort of promotion, confirmation, augmentation, multiplication, or communication.

As Thomas explains that "by blessing is understood not only that you bless with your mouth, but also that you yourself bestow the blessing."[35] When one blesses another, the veracity of such a blessing is twofold: the good desired for another must be truly a good thing, and the minister of the blessing must really desire that good for the other.

There is no morally good blessing if the words used do not manifest what the one who gives the blessing considers to be good or evil. As we already explained, his ignorance or error can also be a matter of moral analysis, because the good that is said to be good must be so in reality.

The same can apply to a curse: "To curse is nothing else but to say evil. I can therefore say that good is evil and evil good, and again, that good is good and evil evil. The first is what the Apostle forbids when he says, *curse not*, i.e., do not say that good is evil and evil good. But the second is lawful."[36]

As we will see, ulterior intentions can further specify the words used in a blessing or in a malediction into different moral species.

MORALITY OF INDICATIVE BLESSINGS

The moral species of a blessing or of a malediction does not require only saying the truth about the good or about evil under their respective formal aspects of good and evil. One must also

---

34. *ST* II–II, q. 76, a. 1, c.
35. *Super Mat.*, c. 15, lect. 1, n. 1290.
36. *Super Gal.*, c. 3, lect. 4, n. 139.

say it with the intention of fostering such good or evil. This last aspect introduces the possibility of distinguishing *formal* blessings and maledictions from blessings and maledictions that are so only *materially*.

Actions that belong to the same species in *genus naturae* can have different species from the viewpoint of the *genus moris*. An indicative blessing directed towards another person could be done to praise that person or to flatter him. A malediction from the material viewpoint could be done to correct someone or to harm him. A false blessing could be so as a lie with the intent to deceive. But it could also be false because it is done, for instance, to manipulate the blessed person through flattery.

Morally Good Indicative Blessings

Morally good indicative blessings are configured as praise or an expression of thanksgiving. Consider for instance how, in Rom 1:25, Paul calls God forever blessed. Aquinas interprets it as follows:

> And for this reason, he adds who is blessed, i.e., whose goodness is evident, just as we are said to bless God, when we admit his goodness with our heart and express it orally: "when you bless him, put forth all your strength" (Eccl 43:30). He adds forever because his goodness is everlasting; it depends on no one else but is the source of all good. For this reason, the worship of *latria* is due him. He ends with amen to indicate absolute certainty: "he who blesses himself in the land shall be blessed by the God of truth" (Isa 65:16). Amen, i.e., it is true, or so be it.[37]

The mention in the text of the *latria* or worship due to God points to the necessary connection between blessings and the virtue of religion, which we will study in our third chapter. For the moment, let us only note that praise manifests with words the goodness of something or someone considered in itself.

---

37. *Super Rom.*, c. 1, lect. 7, n. 144.

Thanksgiving, in turn, adds to this manifestation both the acknowledgement of this goodness as a benefit for the grateful person and the affection toward the benefactor. This expression of gratitude is the beginning of the due reciprocity inherent in the love of the benefactor who has made a good gift out of love.

Praise, properly speaking, is a good moral act. It coincides with the indicative or enunciative blessing. Such a blessing can be directed to God or to other men, and it resembles the love of friendship. Like the latter, indicative blessings can be referred to a good thing, to persons, or to good things that are proper of some persons.

Aquinas explains the different reasons why we address God or other men with words of praise. God already knows our thoughts. But when these words are addressed to other men, they reveal our hearts "in order that he or others may learn that we have a good opinion of him: so that in consequence we may *incite him to yet better things*; and that we may *induce others*, who hear him praised, to think well of him, to reverence him, and *to imitate him*."[38]

The praise of God, in turn, is ordered "not indeed to make known our thoughts to Him Who is the searcher of hearts, but that we may bring ourselves and our hearers to reverence Him."[39]

A blessing is constituted as such in its *genus naturae* as saying the good of what truly is good. In its *genus moris*, a blessing is constituted as such by what we can call its proper end: the fostering of the good. Thus, Aquinas explained, for instance, that we praise someone to incite him to do better things and to encourage others to imitate him.

Morality of Indicative Maledictions

An indicative malediction may also be authentic or false. When we say something evil about someone by lying, we are before a calumny. As we know, such an action is morally wrong.

38. *ST* II–II, q. 91, a. 1, c; emphasis added.

39. *ST* II–II, q. 91, a. 1, c. See also *Super Ps. 27*, n. 252; *Super Iob*, c. 1, lect. 4, n. 36.

When we say something evil about someone and what we say is true, the moral evaluation of the action is more complicated.

Some morally good actions, such as fraternal correction, include these kinds of indicative maledictions. To correct one's brother for whom we desire a good, one needs to tell him the evil he has done. In this case, we have an indicative malediction that, in reality, must be considered as a blessing, because it is ordered to the fostering of the good of the person being corrected.

> To curse is to say something evil. As with blessing, this can happen in three ways, namely, by asserting, by commanding, and by desiring; and in each of these ways something good can be done and something evil. For something materially evil can be called evil in any of these ways. If it is called evil but has a good aspect, this is blessing rather than cursing and is not illicit. For a thing is judged more according to its form than its matter. But if someone says evil under the aspect of evil, he is speaking evil formally; hence it is altogether illicit. Both of these cases occur when someone makes known an evil by asserting it. For sometimes a person asserts that something is evil, in order to make known a necessary truth. Hence, he asserts evil under the aspect of a necessary truth, which is something good; hence it is licit. This is the way Job is said to have cursed his day, when he asserted the evil of the present life (Job 3:1), just as the Apostle did in Ephesians: "making the most of the time, because the days are evil" (Eph 5:17). But sometimes a person asserts someone's evil under the aspect of evil, namely, to detract from his good name; and this is illicit. For it is stated in 1 Corinthians: "the evil-tongued shall not possess God's kingdom" (1 Cor 6:10).[40]

To comment upon and further explain this text, we need to remember that an indicative malediction is open to different intentions which confer the moral species to different sins. Remember how we explained before that form is act and gives the species,

---

40. See *Super Rom.*, c. 12, lect. 3, n. 1000.

and how the willing of the end was like a form, which informs the uttering of the words as matter or object.

In the *Summa Theologiae*, we can read about reviling, backbiting, tale-bearing, etc. These questions are important to comprehend Aquinas' teachings on malediction. But they also serve as examples of how moral actions, which deal with words about another, are specified, mainly because of the intention of the speaking person.

We are now considering the case of someone who says evil of what is evil. Were he to lie, the malediction would automatically be morally wrong for violating the natural end of language. What we are considering here are sins, which must be evaluated depending on the *intention* of the speaking person.[41]

Consider how Thomas summarizes the different intentions that further specify maledictions into different moral species of sins:

> Sins of word should be weighed *chiefly by the intention of the speaker*, wherefore these sins are differentiated according to the various intentions of those who speak against another. Now just as the railer intends to injure the honor of the person he rails, the backbiter to depreciate a good name, and the tale-bearer to destroy friendship, so too the derider intends to shame the person he derides. And since this end is distinct from the others, it follows that the sin of derision is distinct from the foregoing sins.[42]

An action can be specified by different intentions. In fact, one single action can simultaneously have different intentions. But it can also happen that uttering some words may be railing only materially and accidentally. These words may be directed to the good of the other.[43] This malediction would be more of a blessing.

It can also happen that a blessing may be so from the material viewpoint because the intention of the speaking person is not the good of the person being blessed. This is the case of the flatterer.

---

41. See *ST* II–II, q. 73, a. 2, c.

42. *ST* II–II, q. 75, a. 1, c; emphasis added.

43. See *ST* II–II, q. 72, a. 2, c; II–II, q. 73, a. 2, c.

Aquinas offers different examples of how flattery can be contrary to charity. One would be "when a man praises another's sin: for this is contrary to the love of God, against Whose justice he speaks, and contrary to the love of his neighbor, whom he encourages to sin."[44]

This would correspond to the case of the person who blesses with falsity because he praises that which is evil: for instance, to someone blessing homosexual activity or any sexual activity outside of marriage. This praise is against charity because it contradicts love for God since it speaks against his justice. It is also against love of neighbor since it moves him to sin even more. Another example is "when a man flatters another, so that by deceiving him he may injure him in body or in soul."[45]

MORALITY OF IMPERATIVE AND SUBJUNCTIVE BLESSINGS

In its most proper sense, curses are found in imperative and subjunctive maledictions. Their moral consideration can be done together. The acts of wishing and of commanding to do something are correlative with respect to their goodness or badness.

A Formal Curse Is Always Evil

Morally speaking, to curse (*maledicere*), to carry out a formal and essential malediction is always wrong.[46] This malediction consists in ordering or wishing for the evil of another, under the formality of evil, and with the intention of fostering such an evil. For this reason, I have used in the title of this book two imperatives: bless and do not curse. To bless is good *ex genere suo*, and to formally curse is always morally bad.

44. *ST* II–II, q. 115, a. 2, c.

45. *ST* II–II, q. 115, a. 2, c.

46. God never curses us, not even if we end up in hell: "*quia benedictio nostra a Deo est, maledictio autem a nobis.*" *Super Mat.*, c. 25, lect. 3, n. 2107.

The intention of the agent is manifested in the words which express the proper object of cursing as malediction. If what one orders or wishes is something evil but it is willed under the formal aspect of its goodness, insofar as it is good for another, the moral species of the act changes entirely. We do not have a curse anymore but a blessing.

The importance of intention is not to be seen as a sort of intentionalism.[47] The subjective intention of the agent does not change the liceity or lack thereof of the malediction apart from any consideration of the objective evil that is being ordered or wished.

Keep in mind that the evil of guilt (*culpa*), although the first, is not the only analogate of evil. To desire or to command an evil of guilt can never be willed under the formal aspect of goodness. It can never be good in any way. This would amount to commanding someone to sin.

However, the evil of punishment (*poena*) can certainly be willed under the formal aspect of goodness. It can be ordered to the good of another, to the conversion of the one suffering it.[48] A judge can sentence in order to punish a person, who has been found guilty of a crime, with the intent of rehabilitating the perpetrator.[49]

In this case, we would have a *material* malediction. It would not be a malediction formally or essentially speaking, but only *per accidens*. It is more of a blessing than a curse because it is ordered to the real good of the person receiving the punishment.

Imperative Blessings are the Greatest Blessings

These considerations concerning maledictions have their correlate in the question of blessings. The most proper sense of a blessing is found in the imperative blessing. The proper end of blessings, the fostering of the good, is most perfectly present in commands rather than in simple enunciations.

47. See Jensen, *Good and Evil Actions*. See also Brock, "Specification of Action."

48. See *Super Rom.*, c. 12, lect. 3, n. 1002.

49. See *Super Rom.*, c. 12, lect. 3, n. 1001.

Men tend to bless things *acknowledging* their goodness. God blesses creatures by creating their goodness with his command. We love things because they are good. But things are good because God loves and blesses them.[50]

Creation is the first of the Lord's blessings for creatures. No other blessing has meaning or is even possible without this primordial one. God commands with his Word, and things come to be.

An instance of *"benedicere"* or "saying the good" is at the root of each created entity. This same Word sustains the whole created universe in being.[51] God blesses to foster the good, so that created goods may grow, multiply, and diffuse themselves.[52]

The very essence of blessing is most perfectly found in that kind of blessing which has the capacity to generate goodness. Imperative blessings occupy this first place in the gradation of blessings.

The second place goes to subjunctive blessings. They aim at the attainment of a good. The third and last place is for indicative blessings. They limit themselves to acknowledging an already existing good and to foster it by this acknowledgment.

Applying what Aquinas has said about maledictions to the issue of blessings, we must hold that the moral judgment of imperative and subjunctive blessings coincides. This topic is of the utmost importance.

Subjunctive blessings constitute the natural support of Christian prayer of blessing in general. Imperative blessings, in turn, constitute the natural support of Christian blessings as a

---

50. See *ST* I, q. 20, a. 4, c.

51. See *CCC*, 1079.

52. "According to Gregory, the blessing of God signifies the conferral and multiplication of his gifts [*collationem donorum ejus et multiplicationem eorumdem*]" (*In II Sent.*, d. 15, q. 3, a. 3, c). See also *In II Sent.*, d. 18, q. 1, a. 2, sc; *ST* I, q. 72, a. 1, ad 4; *ST* I, q. 73, a. 3, c. God's love is the cause of the being and goodness of things. The entity that has a greater participation in the good has received a greater *blessing*: "*benedictio bonitati debetur*" (*In II Sent.*, d. 15, q. 3, a. 3, sc).

sacramental, performed by the ordained minister as an instrument of Christ, in whose name one blesses with authority.

Coming back to the definition of blessings, we must certainly consider the good that is being ordered, wished, or acknowledged. But we must also look at the intention of the end in the will of the commanding or desiring person, the fostering of the good. This end is the formal principle of the moral object.

One could use words that are materially a blessing with a different intention. A person giving a blessing may know that the formulated good in the blessing is not really a good. But it is also possible that the true good, which is commanded, wished, or acknowledged, may be ulteriorly ordered to an evil. In both cases, we would have only a *material* blessing, a blessing only *per accidens*, something which is more properly a curse.

PERSONS AND "THINGS" AS RECIPIENTS OF BLESSINGS

The Distinction Between Person and "Thing"

Following Boethius's traditional definition, persons are "individual substances of a rational nature."[53] Thus, we can distinguish spiritual substances from any other substance and accident.[54]

Aquinas uses a similar distinction when he asks if we should love irrational creatures with charity. As we will explain, charity is a supernatural love of friendship. Hence, the Angelic Doctor clarifies that "the love of friendship is twofold: first, there is the love for the friend to whom our friendship is given, second, the love for those good things which we desire for our friend."[55]

We cannot love irrational animals with the first love for several reasons. Among them is the fact that irrational creatures are not competent to possess the good. Since they have no free

---

53. *ST* I, q. 29, a. 1, c.

54. See García López, *Tomás de Aquino.*

55. *ST* II–II, q. 25, a. 3, c.

choice, they are not lords over their actions, and they cannot master the disposal of the goods they receive.[56]

Aquinas explains that friendship consists in wishing good things for someone. But we cannot wish good things for a dog, for example. We cannot do so because the dog "is not competent, properly speaking, to possess good, this being proper to the rational creature which, through its free-will, is the master of its disposal of the good it possesses."[57]

To be sure, the word "thing" (*res*) signifies a transcendental property of being, which applies to persons as well. God is a thing! So are you! The reason is very simple: a thing is an entity with an essence.[58] I would even say that God is more a thing than you are. And you are more a thing than an irrational animal is, in the sense that your form or the divine form is more of a form than the form of the cat.

Yet, adopting common parlance, we can distinguish persons who can own or having the good through their free-will from nonspiritual substances and accidents which are not capable of such possession and mastery. They are the object of love in different ways.

Persons are loved with love of friendship. In turn, "things" like a cat or a spiritual quality, like wisdom, are loved with love of concupiscence. We love "things" *for* persons. We love others and ourselves exactly in that way.

Recipients of Blessings

Which persons and things are capable of receiving a blessing? Blessings are a multiform expression of different forms of love. For this reason, they always possess a personal or interpersonal character.

Anything that is truly good is susceptible of an indicative blessing. Things blessed in this way are always referred to a person,

---

56. See Brock, "Aquinas the Conservationist."

57. *ST* II–II, q. 25, a. 3, c.

58. See García López, *Metafísica Tomista.*

at least to the person who blesses them. Their blessing shows that the one performing the blessing considers them to be good.

Moreover, what is acknowledged as good can be acknowledged as such because it is also good for others. Praise and thanksgiving always possess a more or less explicit interpersonal dimension, which combines the love of friendship and the love of concupiscence we just distinguished.

Such a dimension is even more evident in imperative and subjunctive blessings. They are always addressed to intellectual creatures, to persons, to spiritual substances. Entities lacking understanding cannot be the recipient of goods. Non-personal beings are unable to possess them. As Thomas explained, benevolence is a form of love directed toward persons.

Hence, we speak of the blessing of non-personal entities insofar as they are ordered to persons. Good or evil things happen to persons through these kinds of non-personal entities, which colloquially we call "things."

Thus, Aquinas makes the following distinction. On the one hand, "benediction and malediction, properly speaking, regard things to which good or evil may happen, viz. rational creatures."[59] On the other hand, "good and evil are said to happen to irrational creatures in relation to the rational creature for whose sake they are."[60]

Irrational creatures are ordered to persons as a help, as a symbol, and as spatiotemporal framework. God blesses the earth so that it may be fruitful, so that human beings may benefit and satisfy their corporeal needs. There is also at the beginning of creation a malediction of the earth so that man may toil and work as a punishment for original sin. He who is punished through that malediction is man (see Gen 2:17).

Irrational creatures are a symbol. They are important for divine pedagogy. In its own way, the truth of things is a testimony of the First Truth. Through the knowledge of these created things, the human spirit must elevate itself to the knowledge of God.

59. *ST* II–II, q. 76, a. 2, c.
60. *ST* II–II, q. 76, a. 2, c.

Nature is like an open book. God teaches great lessons in it.[61] The first lesson the Lord taught to Adam was precisely through the naming of the animals (see Gen 2:19).[62] The malediction of things can also have this symbolic character. For example, Jesus cursed the fig tree to make a prophetic gesture, to send a message to men (see Matt 21:18–22).

Irrational creatures constitute the spatiotemporal framework wherein man lives. Places and times can be blessed or cursed by different reasons. For example, Job cursed the day he was born so as to curse his contracted original sin and its horrible consequences that he had to suffer (see Job 3:1). His curse was never directed to the gift of life received from God.

Aquinas explicitly considers the indicative blessing of sin (Christian prayer of thanksgiving for sin) as a stupidity or foolishness: "*[No] one can thank God for that which is unlawful. For he is a fool who thanks God for fornication, because God is not the source of evil.*"[63] In this instance, we have a blasphemy. The guilt of sin would now be attributed to God.

This text clears up what Aquinas would think of those who celebrate the alleged discontinuity of *FS* with the previous moral magisterium, as a first step to change the Church's moral teachings concerning homosexuality and eventually bless extramarital sexual activity. The Common Doctor of the Church calls them fools! Moreover, he would also call them blasphemers.

Thomas also notes that "to curse irrational beings, *considered as creatures of God*, is a sin of blasphemy."[64] This last appreciation from Aquinas is important because some detractors of *FS* insist on saying that the blessing of couples in irregular situations is necessarily a blasphemy.

It seems that the text from the Angelic Doctor underscores an important element to be considered in this regard and is greatly

---

61. See John Paul II, *Man and Woman*.

62. See Perez-Lopez, *Procreation*.

63. *Super I Tim.*, c. 4, lect. 1, n. 142; emphasis added. See also *Super Iob*, c. 1, lect. 1, n. 8.

64. *ST* II–II, q. 76, a. 2, c; emphasis added.

forgotten by the lamenters of *FS*, who claim that blessing *couples in irregular unions* is something always wrong and everywhere because it necessarily means the approval of their sinful relationship.

The texts from Thomas make us realize that the blessing or the curse of the same reality could be blasphemy or not, *depending on the formal aspect under which the blessing or the curse is given.*

Our analyses in this book lead us to conclude that the key elements to be considered are the words used (object of the act of blessing) and the intention of the agent who blesses or curses (intention). We will analyze the circumstances in our last chapter dedicated to the virtue of prudence. In this way, we will complete the analysis of the sources of morality of the act of blessing.

We have already talked about the relationship of those words with truth. Of course, that truth as we already said is not the only one available to human reason. It also includes the truth accessible through the light of faith.

We must not forget that veracity is also an infused virtue. The moral truths present in revelation and taught by the Church's magisterium constitute the essential element wherefrom the minister chooses the words of any supernatural blessing in conformity with reality. Every blessing must be truthful because it must conform to the truth revealed in Christ.

It is time to understand how charity must be the main element in that intention and how those words not only must conform to truth, but they must also be a faithful expression of that same charity.

2

Blessings and Charity

THIS SECOND CHAPTER TOUCHES the heart of Aquinas' moral theology of blessings. It centers on the morality of blessings under the light of the virtue of charity. This light is especially present in the manner in which the Angelic Doctor conceives the blessing of sinners, persecutors, and enemies.

However, to reach a solid explanation of the blessing of these people, we need to analyze how Aquinas comments on Rom 12:14, we need to explain the sense in which charity is the form and end of the virtues, why we should pray for our enemies, in what sense charity is friendship with God, and what is charity's motive formal object.

AN INSIGHTFUL "THEOLOGUMENON"

Aquinas' commentary on Rom 12:14 expands on the meaning of the mandate to bless (εὐλογέω) and not curse (καταράομαι) those who persecute (διώκω) us. This commentary is the most articulated text found in the *corpus thomisticum* concerning our topic.

Thomas interprets verses 14–21 as follows: "The Apostle showed that charity should be practiced toward the needy; now he shows how *it should be practiced even toward enemies*."[1]

The mandate to bless and not curse is framed, by Aquinas' text, within the benevolence toward one's enemies inherent in charity. Christian blessings are presented, therefore, as an exterior effective expression of the affective supernatural love proper to the queen of virtues.[2]

I propose that the study of this connection is the key doctrinal *theologumenon* to understand who and what can be blessed, and in which way such a blessing must be performed. It is the key to interpret *FS* in continuity with previous magisterium and sound doctrine, avoiding the hermeneutics of suspicion previously mentioned.

Charity is the only virtue that immediately sanctifies.[3] Acts of other virtues are meritorious, relevant to attain eternal life, only in the measure in which they are animated by charity.[4]

Human acts are meritorious because of two things. First, because of "the Divine ordination, inasmuch as acts are said to merit that good to which man is divinely ordained."[5]

Second, human acts are meritorious "on the part of free-will, inasmuch as man, more than other creatures, has the power of voluntary acts by acting by himself."[6] Thomas concludes that "in both these ways does merit chiefly rest with charity."[7]

Without charity, we are simply nothing (see 1 Cor 13). Charity is the queen, mother, root, form, and soul of all Christian virtues.[8]

---

1. *Super Rom.*, c. 12, lect. 3, n. 996; emphasis added. See also *Super I Cor.*, c. 4, lect. 2, n. 217.

2. *Super Rom.*, c. 12, lect. 3, n. 997.

3. This thesis is proven by Antonio Royo Marín. See Royo Marín, *Theology of Christian Perfection*. See also Royo Marín, *Teología Moral Para Seglares*.

4. See Royo Marín, *Teología de la Caridad*.

5. *ST* I–II, q. 114, a. 4, c.

6. *ST* I–II, q. 114, a. 4, c.

7. *ST* I–II, q. 114, a. 4, c.

8. See *ST* II–II, q. 23, a. 8.

Christian blessings are good, holy, and meritorious if they can be commanded, engendered, nourished, and informed by charity.

The contrary must also be true. If a blessing cannot be informed by charity, such a blessing must be a morally bad Christian blessing. This principle does not apply to formal and essential maledictions since these are always evil and illicit. But it can have a certain application to material maledictions, such as fraternal correction.[9] Maledictions of this kind are more of a blessing. They are ordered to the good of our neighbor.

Christian blessings possess a deep connection with Christ's charity, the Good Shepherd, and Eternal High Priest.[10]

The most excellent virtues extend their influx by governing others. At the top of the *human* virtues, we have the virtue of religion which relates us with God as servants who worship him. Its excellence is manifested in its capacity to command the acts of other virtues offered to God as sacrifice.

Charity is greater than religion since it unites us with God as his sons and friends.[11] This friendship is so intimate that it is illustrated by the spousal analogy. Marriage, as conjugal friendship, is the most intimate form of friendship possible between a man and a woman. In charity, the church is presented as Christ's bride. For this reason, the church is Christ's body, because she is united to him through this intimate love of conjugal friendship.

CHARITY AS THE FORM AND END OF THE VIRTUES

Understanding Aquinas' moral theology of Christian blessings leads us to envision the act of blessing as an act in which charity commands the virtues of veracity, religion, and prudence. But this

---

9. See *ST* II–II, q. 33, a. 1.

10. See Torrell, *Christ and Spirituality*.

11. See *ST* II–II, q. 23, a. 1.

command is best comprehended when we study the way in which charity is the form and end of the virtues.[12]

Aquinas holds that charity is the form of the other virtues and of their acts. He escapes the error of thinking that all virtues are nothing but charity.[13] The latter is not their essential form. Charity is not the form of the virtues the way the soul of Socrates is his substantial form. Yet, there is a certain sense in which charity is their exemplar.

Is Charity an Exemplary Form?

At first glance, our last affirmation is at odds with Aquinas. It would seem that charity cannot be considered as the exemplary form of the virtues. There is a text from the *Summa Theologiae* that could lead the superficial reader to this position: "Charity is called the form of the other virtues not as being their exemplar or their essential form, but rather by way of efficient cause, insofar as it sets the form on all, in the aforesaid manner."[14]

However, a careful reading of the context of this reply leads to a different conclusion. Charity is a special kind of exemplary form. It is not an exemplary form like the original in imitation of which something is made. Rather, charity is an exemplary form like "that according to the likeness of which something is made and through participation in which it has being."[15]

The exemplarity of charity is, in fact, in harmony with the way of the efficient cause mentioned in the text.

Aquinas teaches, offering a certain innovation with respect to Peter Lombard, that the formation of lower virtues does not come directly from grace. It is mediated by higher virtues.[16]

---

12. For this section, I am drawing from Perez-Lopez, "Thomas Aquinas."

13. See *ST* II–II, q. 23, a. 4.

14. See *ST* II–II, q. 23, a. 8, ad 1. For a more comprehensive treatment of this question, see Falanga, *Charity*.

15. *In III Sent.*, d. 27, q. 2, a. 4, qc. 3, ad 1.

16. See *De Verit.*, q. 14, a. 5, c.

The key here will be a *theology and a metaphysics of participation*.[17] Thomas views the effect due to the higher agent as formal, while that which comes from the lower agent as material.[18] Lower virtues participate in the perfection of higher ones. But they do so in a special manner, after the mode of being of the former.

In a virtue of a lower power, we can refer to "a certain form by which it is constituted a virtue owing to its participation in a higher power's perfection."[19]

Consider the following example. Prudence makes moral virtues to be virtues. Prudence is an *exemplary* form to the virtues such as temperance. But we can also speak of a different essential form in temperance.[20] This other intrinsic form makes the virtue in question to have a distinct species according to the principle already explained, *forma dat speciem.*

The act of this virtue is impacted by these *two* forms. Thus, infused temperance "places into its act a manner of acting proper to temperance, as well as that which it has from prudence, from charity, and from grace."[21]

In reality, Thomas is applying here a metaphysical principle he has carefully developed in the *Prima Pars* of the *Summa Theologiae*, where he discussed his metaphysics of participation of created goods in the Divine Good, with a certain influence from Dionysius the Areopagite.[22]

> Whatever perfection exists in an effect must be found in the effective cause: either in the same formality, if it is a univocal agent—as when man reproduces man; or in a more eminent degree, if it is an equivocal agent—thus

---

17. See Fabro, *Nozione Metafisica de Partecipazione*. See also Te Velde, *Participation and Substantiality*.

18. See *De Verit.*, q. 14, a. 5, c. See also *In III Sent.*, d. 27, q. 2, a. 4, qc. 3, ad 2.

19. *In III Sent.*, d. 27, q. 2, a. 4, qc. 3, ad 5.

20. See *In III Sent.*, d. 27, q. 2, a. 4, qc. 3, ad 5.

21. *In III Sent.*, d. 27, q. 2, a. 4, qc. 3, ad 5.

22. For the way in which this author influences Aquinas' metaphysics, see Andereggen, *Filosofía Primera*.

in the sun is the likeness of whatever is generated by the sun's power. Now it is plain that the effect pre-exists virtually in the efficient cause: and although to pre-exist in the potentiality of a material cause is to pre-exist in a more imperfect way, since matter as such is imperfect, and an agent as such is perfect; still to pre-exist virtually in the efficient cause is to pre-exist not in a more imperfect, but in a more perfect way. Since therefore God is the first effective cause of things, the perfections of all things must pre-exist in God in a more eminent way.[23]

Created goods participate in the perfection of divine goodness. The latter is their *exemplary* form. Created goods depend in being on the divine goodness. But created goods remain distinct from divine goodness. These goods are not divine.

> Some things are said to be alike which communicate in the same form, but not according to the same formality; as we see in non-univocal agents. For since every agent reproduces itself so far as it is an agent, and everything acts according to the manner of its form, the effect must in some way resemble the form of the agent.[24]

Similarly, moral virtues *participate* in the perfection of prudence. Moral virtues communicate in the same form but not according to the same formality. They depend on prudence for their being virtues. But they do so without becoming prudence.

They are sealed by moral wisdom. Yet, they do not become intellectual. They do not lose their own identity. The effect of the *equivocal* agent as efficient cause is of a different nature than the cause. But it participates in the being of the cause, and it imitates as much as it can that same cause.

Aquinas uses these same principles to explain why charity is included in the very definition of the human virtues within the supernatural order: "Charity is the form that causes the notion of virtue to be perfectly realized in each and every virtue."[25] Hence, the

---

23. *ST* I, q. 4, a. 2, c.

24. *ST* I, q. 4, a. 3, c.

25. *In III Sent.*, d. 27, q. 2, a. 4, qc. 3, c. See also *In II Sent.*, d. 41, q. 1, a. 1, c.

same reasoning process I have presented about prudence applies to charity as the highest virtue that engenders all the lower ones.

The End, Mover, and Mother

Charity is the end and mover of the virtues. It commands their acts because charity "calls all the acts of the virtues together to their end by the fact that its object is the last end."[26]

All the acts of God's commandments and consequently, all the acts of the human virtues, find their completion in charity: "Love is the fulfilling of the law" (Rom 13:10). As a result, charity is the end of the virtues. The latter are, at the same time, ends in themselves and a *means* to charity.

Charity is also *their mover* because, "the good itself, which is charity's object under the notion of final end, is the [common] end of the virtues. But in all powers or arts of a single order, it happens that the art or power that has to do with the ultimate end orders the acts of other arts or powers to their proper ends, as the military art, which exists for the sake of victory (to which every particular military task is ordered), orders the equestrian and naval arts to their ends."[27]

Charity leads to heaven as the perfection of Christian life. It moves and commands the other virtues similarly to the way in which a higher art commands and governs a lower one.[28] Thus, charity is "common to all the virtues by reason of the diffusion of its governance."[29]

Charity is also the *mother and root* of the virtues since it engenders in her womb the other virtues. Precisely because we will to love God, we conceive and perform acts of veracity, religion, prudence, etc. Since there is no higher virtue than charity, the

---

26. *In II Sent.*, d. 26, q. 1, a. 4, ad 5.
27. *In III Sent.*, d. 27, q. 2, a. 4, qc. 3, c.
28. See *In I Ethic.*, lect. 2, n. 25.
29. *De Malo*, q. 8, a. 2, c.

formation of the lower virtues should take place through charity's motherhood.[30]

PRAYING FOR OUR ENEMIES

We are interested in showing how the virtue of charity is the exemplary form of the virtue of religion. More concretely, we want to focus on the act of prayer and the blessings therein included.

In the *Summa Theologiae*, Aquinas explains that we should pray for our enemies. Therein, we find again the connection between charity and prayer. Their objects are coextensive: "To pray for another is an act of charity, as stated above. Wherefore we are bound to pray for our enemies in the same manner as we are bound to love them."[31]

In this text, we find a clear application of the insightful *theologumenon* that Aquinas indicates in his commentary on Rom 12:14. We are bound to love our enemies. We must not love their sin. But we must love them in general and be spiritually prepared to love them individually when the case arises: "To love one's enemies absolutely in the individual, and to assist them, is an act of perfection."[32]

Consequently, to elevate our minds to the Lord to ask for them fitting things cannot be an evil act. On the contrary, sometimes it is obligatory. Other times, it is a matter of perfection: "It is a matter of obligation that we should not exclude our enemies from the general prayers which we offer up for others: but it is a matter of perfection, and not of obligation, to pray for them individually, except in certain special cases."[33]

What special cases does Thomas have in mind? Is he referring to unrepentant sinners? To elucidate this question, we need to deepen our understanding of his theology of charity.

30. See *In III Sent.*, d. 27, q. 2, a. 4, qc. 3, c.
31. *ST* II–II, q. 83, a. 8, c.
32. *ST* II–II, q. 83, a. 8, c.
33. *ST* II–II, q. 83, a. 8, c.

"AMICITIA CARITATIS" AND CHRISTIAN BLESSINGS

Friendship is a form of benevolent love. It is reciprocal and reciprocally conscious. It is founded upon a communication of goods, namely, a common good.[34] This common good is God himself, his eternal and blessed life. The Lord invites us to become his friends by sharing with us his infinite goodness.

Friends share life. Charity is a familial conversation with God. In sharing their life, spiritual beings share their secrets, their minds, and their hearts. This supernatural friendship is a friendship in Christ.

The Holy Spirit communicates the life of grace to us as a participation in Christ's divine life. We become sons in the Son. Jesus reveals to us the Father's secrets. Our friendship with Christ leads us to think, to love, and to feel in harmony with his Sacred Heart, because friends are "another I," in this case, *alter Christus*.

The Christian who leads the life of grace and possesses charity is called to express the benevolence inherent in this supernatural love *through his words of blessing*. Hence, Christian blessings must be a manifestation of the same heart of Christ with which the Christian is configured and conformed. "Love one another as I have loved you" (John 13:34). "Remain in my love" (John 15:9). Christ's charity must be the measure of charity. Hence, it must also be the measure of Christian blessings.

What is first in each genus is the measure of this genus. If we speak about charity, uncreated charity, God himself, is the source of all charity. Divine love is the source of the love of charity, which abounds in the human will of Christ. God is the one who saves and communicates grace. But the humanity of Christ is the instrumental cause of salvation, the conjoined instrument by virtue of the hypostatic union.

By the grace of union of Christ's human nature with the divine nature in the Person of the Word, Jesus came to this world

---

34. See Ramírez, *De Caritate*, 38–39.

full of grace and truth, and from his fullness, we have received grace upon grace (see John 1:14, 16).

The first born among the dead is the measure of the new man. The Aristotelian thesis according to which the virtuous man is the measure of all things reaches, in Christ's humanity, an unsuspected depth.

The charity of every Christian is necessarily a participation and an imitation of Christ's charity. Through the action of the Holy Spirit, Christ's charity is poured out as a chrism that goes from the Head to each of the members of the church.

Aquinas' treatise on charity is a theological immersion in Christ's heart, wherein we find created charity in its perfect and exemplary state. We cannot go over the whole treatise here. I am limiting myself to the explanation of some basic elements for the question of Christian blessings.

BEYOND SHEER PHILANTHROPY: CHARITY'S MOTIVE FORMAL OBJECT

We need to move beyond our contemporary reduction of charity to philanthropy. The latter is human while the former is divine. Someone may object to this position by arguing that charity includes our neighbor. Hence, it seems that there is a charity that is essentially philanthropic.

Moreover, it would seem that there are two kinds of charity, one directed to the love of God and another to the love of one's neighbor. Virtues are specified by their objects. How could charity be one in its species since charity extends to both God and neighbor? Different objects seem to require different kinds of charity.

We need to pay close attention to the following text from the *Summa Theologiae*. Aquinas has already explained what we covered before, namely, that charity is friendship with God. He takes a look at how friendships are specified to investigate if charity is one or if it has different species.

There are two main ways in which friendships are differentiated. The first one deals with the diversity of their ends: "in this way there are three species of friendship, namely friendship for the useful, for the delightful, and for the virtuous."[35]

In turn, the second concentrates on the different kinds of communions or *communicatio* on which friendships are based: "thus there is one species of friendship between kinsmen, and another between fellow citizens or fellow travelers, the former being based on natural communion, the latter on civil communion or on the comradeship of the road."[36]

None of these apply to charity. The first does not apply because charity has only one end: God's goodness. The second does not apply either because the *communicatio* at the heart of charity is also one: fellowship in eternal or divine life. For this reason, Thomas concludes that "charity is simply one virtue, and not divided into several species."[37]

What about the objection based on the different objects of charity? Aquinas solves this question by appealing to the metaphysical teaching according to which form specifies (*forma dat speciem*).

There is only one motive formal object in charity, also in the act directed to one's neighbor: God himself in his infinite goodness and eternal blessedness. The argument presented concerning the different objects of charity (God and neighbor) "would hold, if God and our neighbor were equally objects of charity. But this is not true: for God is the principal object of charity, while our neighbor is loved out of charity for God's sake."[38]

There are not different species of charity when we love different things or persons. What moves the love of charity for one's neighbor and for those goods that are for him is the love for God.

Thus, charity is the ultimate *ordo amoris*. It confers an order to all loves of friendship and concupiscence that exist within the heart of the Christian. The governance that charity exercises over theological hope and over the other virtues makes charity's influx extend to all the loves of the Christian.

---

35. *ST* II–II, q. 23, a. 5, c.
36. *ST* II–II, q. 23, a. 5, c.
37. *ST* II–II, q. 23, a. 5, c.
38. See *ST* II–II, q. 23, a. 5, ad 1.

This doctrine on the motive formal object in charity sheds light on what is loved with this virtue. We love God, oneself, and our neighbor, including here sinners and enemies. Moreover, in charity we also love grace and charity itself, as the goods *par excellence* desired for oneself and for others. Even irrational beings are also loved with charity because they give glory to God and are useful to men.

Yet, in charity, everything and everyone is loved because of God and for God. Other persons and things are loved because of what we find in them of God. They are loved for the glory and honor of the Father.

Following the connection made by Aquinas in his *Commentary on Romans*, since we must have charity for our neighbor, we must also bless our neighbor. But what is the formal aspect under which we should bless them? We should bless anyone who is our neighbor, and our blessing should be a faithful expression of charity.

My neighbor is any spiritual creature who is an actual or potential member of the communion of saints. All human persons, in the state of wayfarers (*viatores*), are potential members of Christ's body. All of them are lovable with charity. Christian blessings, as a faithful expression of this charity, must be extended to *all* of them.

Aquinas explains the notion used here as a potential member of the communion of saints when he deals with the question of Christ as the Head of *all* men. He begins distinguishing a natural body from the Church's mystical body.

In a natural body, the members are all together. This is not the case in the mystical body of the church. The latter is composed of men and women from different ages.

Moreover, these men and women were at some point in the state of grace and other times not: "Of those who are at any one time, some there are who are without grace, yet will afterwards obtain it, and some have it already. We must therefore consider the members of the mystical body not only as they are in act, but as they are in *potentiality*."[39]

39. *ST* III, q. 8, a. 3, c.

The expression of the blessing granted to every potential member of the communion of saints must be faithful. The words of blessing must reflect what is loved and why it is loved in Christian charity.

We must make a foundational distinction in sinners. On the one hand, we have their nature, through which they are *capax Dei*. On the other hand, we have their evil of guilt (*culpa*), because of which they are not united in actuality with God in the state of grace: "It is our duty to hate, in the sinner, his being a sinner, and to love in him, his being a man capable of bliss; and this is to love him truly, out of charity, for God's sake."[40]

What makes the sinner to be a sinner cannot be the object of either charity or blessing. It must be the object of malediction. Instead, what makes us *capax Dei* and potential members of the communion of saints can and must be the object of charity and of blessings, especially with the kind of ascending blessings of praise and thanksgiving to the Creator. Furthermore, one must ask for the graces needed for those being blessed to be freed from sin and be brought unto eternal life.

Charity moves Christians to be more favorable to those who are more lost and are not yet capable of conversion. Like the Good Shepherd, we need to look for the lost sheep.[41]

Christian blessings should also reflect this aspect of charity, especially through a prayer of intercession. It is not a matter of loving sinners by adopting a worldly mentality contrary to the Gospel. Such a love would not be in consonance with Christ's love. It would not be charity.

> We love sinners out of charity, not so as to will what they will, or to rejoice in what gives them joy, but so as to make them will what we will and rejoice in what rejoices us. Hence it is written (Jer 15:19): "They shall be turned to thee, and thou shalt not to be turned to them."[42]

---

40. *ST* II–II, q. 25, a. 6, c.
41. See *ST* II–II, q. 25, a. 6, ad 2.
42. *ST* II–II, q. 25, a. 6, ad 4.

Ordained ministers such as priests and deacons must already possess a state of perfection that allows them to associate with sinners to seek their conversion. This is the perspective from which they are asked to bless them.

> The weak should avoid associating with sinners, on account of the danger in which they stand of being perverted by them. But it is commendable for the perfect, of whose perversion there is no fear, to associate with sinners that they may convert them. For thus did Our Lord eat and drink with sinners as related by Matt. 9:11–13. Yet all should avoid the society of sinners, as regards fellowship in sin; in this sense it is written (2 Cor 6:17): "Go out from among them . . . and touch not the unclean thing, i.e., by consenting to sin."[43]

A blessing that expresses a love which adopts a worldly mentality characteristic of sinners would never be a Christian blessing. A blessing that wills what sinners will and rejoices in that which they rejoice is *never* animated by charity. Celebrants of the alleged discontinuity of *FS* should take good note of this conclusion.

Our enemies are not loved in charity because of their enmity. We do not love their malice or their sinfulness. To do so would make us wicked. It would never make us saints.

What is loved in our enemies is the image of God through which they are still potential members of the communion of saints. What moves the heart of the Christian to love his enemies is precisely his own friendship with God and the potential friendship his enemy may have with the Lord.[44] Without these motives or reasons, there is no charity.

LOVING AND BLESSING SINNERS

According to the Angelic Doctor, to be loved with charity, we cannot require from our enemies and persecutors the antecedent

43. *ST* II–II, q. 25, a. 6, ad 5.

44. See *ST* II–II, q. 25, a. 8, c.

condition to show repentance. If we want to follow Christ's teachings, we cannot tell our enemies, "If you do not repent, I will not love you."

That is not the position of either Aquinas or Jesus. The Angelic Doctor is crystal clear in his explanation of the teachings of Christ: "One who repents and seeks forgiveness should no longer be reckoned an enemy or persecutor."[45] And Christ has explicitly commanded us to love our *enemies*, just as he loved us when we were his enemies, namely, not when we had already repented, but rather when we still were sinners (see Matt 5:43–44; Luke 6:27–28; Rom 5:8; 1 Pet 3:9).

By enemies and persecutors, we mean impenitent and unrepentant persons. These people are not yet ready to ask for mercy. Nevertheless, we must love them, and we must bless them. The explicit divine commandment found in Rom 12:14 includes them. Bless and do not curse!

In fact, blessing sinners is traditional Church practice. The *Catena Aurea* records the following commentary from John Chrysostom on Christ's saying concerning pearls given to the swine:

> With good reason He forbade pearls to be given to swine. For if they are not to be set before swine that are the less unclean, how much more are they to be withheld from dogs that are so much more unclean. But respecting the giving of that which is holy, we cannot hold the same opinion; seeing *we often give the benediction to Christians who live as the brutes; and that not because they deserve to receive it,* but lest perchance being more grievously offended they should perish utterly.[46]

The text is clear. It records the custom of the ancient Church and of our tradition. We have always blessed sinners, even those who do not deserve the blessing.

Is anyone then excluded from the love of charity and consequently from blessings? Avoiding Manicheism, we must

---

45. "Ille autem qui poenitet et misericordiam petit, iam non est inter inimicos aut persecutores computandus" (*Super Rom.*, c. 12, lect. 3, n. 998).

46. *Catena in Mt.*, c. 7, lect. 3; emphasis added.

remember that everything created by God has a certain participated goodness.[47] Yet, demons, for example, must not be loved with charity. They cannot be redeemed. They must not be our friends.

God has justly condemned demons forever. We rejoice in divine justice and mercy.[48] To think that we would have been more merciful with them than God is crazy and contains a hypocrisy difficult to express. To be the friend of demons would oppose charity.

However, not even the fallen angel we call "the evil one" is pure evil. We must distinguish in every fallen angel his good created nature, made in God's image, from his guilt.

> In the devil both nature and guilt must be considered. His nature indeed is good and is from God nor is it lawful to curse it. On the other hand, his guilt is deserving of being cursed, according to Job 3:8: "Let them curse it who curse the day." Yet when a sinner curses the devil on account of his guilt, for the same reason he judges himself worthy of being cursed; and in this sense he is said to curse his own soul.[49]

To curse demons, insofar as they are God's creatures, is to incur the sin of blasphemy. We cannot be their friends. But we cannot deny their natural goodness. The only way demons can be the object of charity is the way in which irrational creatures fall under this virtue.

This kind of love for them consists in willing that with their condemnation, they give glory to the Father, and that they may be useful to other intellectual creatures, who participate or are called to participate in the communion of saints.

> In this way we love irrational creatures out of charity, inasmuch as we wish them to endure, to give glory to God and be useful to man, as stated above: and in this way too we can love the nature of the demons even out of

47. See *Super I Tim.*, c. 4, lect. 1, nn. 137–48.
48. See *ST* II–II, q. 25, a. 11, c.
49. *ST* II–II, q. 76, a. 1, ad 4.

charity, inasmuch as we desire those spirits to endure, as to their natural gifts, unto God's glory.[50]

Christian blessings must manifest with words the charity which orders the loves of our heart in complete harmony with the heart of Good Shepherd. The mandate to bless, addressed to all followers of Christ, commands benevolence and prayer for all the potential members of the communion of saints, without excluding sinners or enemies.

The formal reason (*ratio formalis*) of this blessing must coincide with the formal reason of charity. Sinners must be blessed for what they have of God in them and not because of their sins.

Christian blessings must ask for them the necessary means for their conversion and sanctification. The key elements to judge the morality of blessings are both their proximate object (the words of the blessing) and the end of the will of the agent. There must be a hylomorphic proportion, coadaptation, or commensuration between the words (matter) and the charitable benevolence (form). This coadaptation is best studied in light of the virtue of religion.

---

50. *ST* II–II, q. 25, a. 11, c.

3

Blessings and Religion

THE THOMISTIC TEACHING CONCERNING prayer, within the sphere of the virtue of religion and animated by charity, has great value in shedding further light on the commensuration between the affections of the heart and the words used in the prayer of blessing. As it was explained, these two elements together with the circumstances constitute the sources of the morality of the deliberate act of blessing another.

In this chapter, we will study the nature of the virtue of religion, the natural structure of petitions inherent in subjunctive blessings, the nature of blessings as sacramentals, a fuller and more complete taxonomy of blessings, and the evaluation of blessings under the light of vices against religion such as blasphemy, sacrilege, and simony.

NOMINAL DEFINITION OF RELIGION

As we did in the first chapter with the term "blessing," we must begin our analysis of religion by clarifying its nominal definition. In this case, we need to concentrate on two interrelated terms: religion and piety.

The English word "piety" comes from the Latin "*pietas*" and from the Greek "εὐσέβεια." Yet, piety also signifies what is meant by "*religio*," *latria*, and "Θεοσέβεια."[1] Both terms are closely connected.

Thomas explains this interrelation making a reference to obedience. He explains that "some special and supreme mode [of obedience] is owed to God, because in Him is the supreme reason of majesty and lordship."[2]

We call this supreme mode of obedience piety, "inasmuch as it is ordered toward the bringing about of devotion."[3] Moreover, we also refer to it as Θεοσέβεια (divine worship) or εὐσέβεια (good worship), as "it is ordered toward an attentive intention."[4] We call it *latria* or service, because "it is ordered toward works in recognition of God's lordship, works that are suitable to Him from the law of creation."[5]

This same virtue "is also called religion insofar as it is ordered toward the determination of works to which man determines himself by binding himself in God's worship."[6]

The origin of the word "religion" is uncertain. We have at least two good options. It could find its root in the verb "*relegit*," literally, "to read again." Thus, religion would be all about reading again the things which pertain to God's worship, because we ought to frequently ponder these things in our hearts.[7]

However, religion could also come from "*religare*," to bind together or to bind again.[8] Thus, religion would be all about binding ourselves to God, clinging to him as our last end.

Be that as it may, we are dealing here with our relationship with God. Religion or piety direct the human person to him.

---

1. I am drawing here from Perez-Lopez, *Priest as a Man of Justice*, 227–32.

2. *In III Sent.*, d. 9, q. 1, a. 2, qc. 1, c.

3. *In III Sent.*, d. 9, q. 1, a. 2, qc. 1, c.

4. *In III Sent.*, d. 9, q. 1, a. 2, qc. 1, c. See *ST* II–II, q. 80, a. 1, ad 4.

5. *In III Sent.*, d. 9, q. 1, a. 2, qc. 1, c.

6. *In III Sent.*, d. 9, q. 1, a. 2, qc. 1, c.

7. See Prov 3:6; *ST* II–II, q. 81, a. 1, c.

8. See *SCG* III, 119.

Religion binds man to God as his most radical principle and final end.

As we know, lordship belongs to God in this supreme way.[9] No one has God's excellence, and no one bestows gifts on us like God. Lordship belongs to God in a unique way. He is the Creator. He governs all things and has dominion over them.

God is "the Alpha and the Omega, the first and the last, the beginning and the end."[10] Religion is a tribute to these truths. "Consequently, a special kind of service is due to Him, which is known as *latria* in Greek; and therefore it belongs to religion."[11]

Religion makes us grow in the awareness of the Psalmist's words: "Know that the Lord is God! It is he that made us, and we are his; we are his people, and the sheep of his pasture."[12]

The Second Vatican Council has clearly taught that only in the sincere gift of self to God does our life find its true meaning.[13] Such a gift, especially when it is informed by charity, is another way of expressing the service and worship that is due to him as our Father.

Those who belong to religious orders manifest in a visible and special way the religious character which belongs to the life of every Christian.[14] It is obvious that not all religious men and women are holy. But it is equally evident that every holy man or woman is religious, whether he or she belongs to an order or not.

We should all give ourselves in sacrifice for God, thereby imitating Christ's sacrificial self-offering for the church.[15] We should all make of our lives a spiritual host.[16]

Such an offering commands acts of other virtues as well. For instance, when a person studies theology, by having a

9. See *ST* II–II, q. 81, a. 1, ad 3.

10. Rev 22:13.

11. *ST* II–II, q. 81, a. 1, ad 3. See Farrell, *Fullness of Life*, 252.

12. Ps 100:3.

13. See *GS*, 24.

14. See *ST* II–II, q. 81, a. 1, ad 5.

15. See Eph 5:25.

16. See Rom 12:1.

religious attitude, he can thus perform an elicit act of the virtue of studiousness, but also a commanded sacrificial act of religion. This sacrificial act, in turn, can also be informed by charity.[17]

WHAT SHALL I RENDER TO THE LORD FOR ALL HIS BOUNTY TO ME?

Religion is a potential part or an annexed virtue to justice. The former resembles, to a degree, the latter. Like justice, religion is ordered to another, and it deals with a legal debt. Unlike justice, in religion, one cannot exactly repay what is received.

> There are certain virtues by which one renders to another what he owes him by the necessity of the law, yet not as much [as he owes him], since this is impossible; for example, in the honor that is owed to God, which religion gives, and that which is owed one's parents and fatherland, which piety gives. Whence these virtues fall short of justice, and are its potential parts, and stand nearest to it.[18]

As the Psalmist says, "What shall I render to the Lord for all his bounty to me?"[19] Religion's debt is one of *inequality*.[20] "Whatever man renders to God is due, yet it cannot be equal, as though man rendered to God as much as he owes Him."[21]

A person becomes another's debtor in different ways, depending on the other's excellence and on the diverse benefits received from him.[22] Religion is directly concerned with God. It deals with God's excellence and with the favors he bestows on us in his providence and government, as our supreme and most radical principle of being and conduct, and as our final end.

17. See *ST* II–II, q. 81, a. 1, ad 1.
18. *In III Sent.*, d. 33, q. 3, a. 4, qc. 1, c.
19. Ps 116:12.
20. See *ST* II–II, q. 80, a. 4, ad 3.
21. *ST* II–II, q. 80, a. 1, c.
22. See *ST* II–II, q. 101, a. 1, c.

There is a unique service and worship that is owed to God's lordship. Such service and worship is closely linked not only with the Holy Spirit's gift of piety but also with that of fear of the Lord. In the latter, we reverence God in the contemplation of his perfection and our imperfection.[23]

However, we must clear up a potential misunderstanding. God is not the direct object but the end of religion. The latter is not a *theological* virtue. Religion is about the debt owed to God and the actions by which we serve and worship him.[24]

The Lord is to be worshipped with both internal acts of the heart and external actions that have to do with corporeal things. We do not pay worship to God because he needs it or because it adds anything to him. We worship him for our own sake: "because by the very fact that we revere and honor God, *our mind is subjected to Him*; wherein its perfection consists, since a thing is perfected by being subjected to its superior."[25]

This observation is important when we approach the topic of blessings. As an act of religion, every blessing must express the subjection of our mind to the Lord. It entails a certain obedience to him.

We bless what he blesses and how he blesses. His explicit command to bless even our persecutors, namely, to bless all potential members of the communion of saints must be kept in mind, if we want to be religious and pious.

We worship God so that our heart, mind, or spirit (*mens*) may be subjected to him. In this sense, we are to worship God in spirit and truth. True worship is a movement in which our heart is in harmony with God.

As Thomas explains, religion "consists in the act whereby we worship God by subjecting ourselves to Him. This act ought to be in harmony with the one who is worshipped and with the one who does the worshipping. Now, He who is worshipped, being a spirit, cannot be contacted by the body but only by the spirit [*mens*].

23. See *De Virtutibus*, q. 4, a. 4, ad 2; *ST* II–II, q. 80, a. 2, ad 1.

24. See *ST* II–II, q. 80, a. 4, c, ad 2.

25. *ST* II–II, q. 81, a. 7, c.

Consequently, his adoration consists chiefly in the act of the heart [*mens*], by which the mind [*mens*] is oriented to God."[26]

Considered in themselves and according to their own importance or value, the internal acts of religion take precedence over the external ones. However, we are rational animals whose knowledge and love begins with sensible things.

We need visible signs of invisible realities: "It is connatural for man to receive knowledge through his senses, and since it is very difficult to transcend sensible objects, divine provision has been made for man so that a reminder of divine things might be made for him, even in the order of sensible things."[27]

God has offered this help so that "the intention of man might be better recalled to divine matters, even in the case of the man whose mind is not strong enough to contemplate divine things in themselves. And it was for this reason that sensible sacrifices were instituted."[28]

Thus, in the pedagogical order of generation, the external acts of religion come first.[29] For this reason, Aquinas explains that "the human mind, in order to be united to God, needs to be guided by the sensible world."[30]

Good and beautiful liturgy, for instance, is foundational. The use of corporeal things at the liturgy is meant to elicit all the interior acts of religion. It is meant to help us grow in devotion and prayer. Blessings, therefore, are instruments of teaching and should lead to an increase of our devotion.

For this reason, it is part of the virtue of religion to take good care of the liturgy in general and of liturgical blessings in particular. Liturgy, without the internal acts of religion, is empty and hypocritical. However, liturgy is also the pedagogue that elicits devotion, prayer, and ultimately, union with God.

26. *Super De Trinitate*, q. 3, a. 2, c. See also John 4:24; *ST* II–II, q. 81, a. 7, ad 1.

27. *SCG* III, 119.

28. *SCG* III, 119.

29. See *De Civitate Dei*, X, 5.

30. *ST* II–II, q. 81, a. 7, c.

As the Angelic Doctor explains, "in the Divine worship it is necessary to make use of corporeal things, that man's mind may be aroused thereby, as by signs, to the spiritual acts by means of which he is united to God. Therefore, the internal acts of religion take precedence of the others and belong to religion essentially, while its external acts are secondary, and subordinate to the internal acts."[31]

One could even say that the external acts of blessing sinners, in the way God blesses and loves them, is a pedagogical tool, which sensibly teaches the members of the church to be subordinated to God, to worship him with devotion and with that mercy and not sheer external sacrifice Jesus mentions in the Gospel (see Matt 9:13).

What should we render to the Lord for all the good things he has done for us? At least, we should be merciful, especially with those whose misery or sins prevent them from being actual and spiritually living members of the church. Bless and do not curse them!

NATURAL STRUCTURE OF PETITIONS AND THE FOUR ELEMENTS OF PRAYER

Prayer is an act of religion. It can be understood in three deeply interrelated ways. The broadest sense of prayer is the elevation of the mind to God that is proper to any of the acts of the theological virtues. A more restricted sense designates any acts of divine worship proper to the act of religion. Lastly, the strictest sense of prayer is the elevation of the mind to God to ask fitting things of him.[32] Thus understood, prayer is an act of practical reason.[33] It belongs to a subjunctive form of discourse. Petition is at its center.

Human reason can discover order. But it is also able to give orders, to command. The contemplative gaze of the intellect

---

31. *ST* II–II, q. 81, a. 7, c. See also *Super De Trinitate*, q. 3, a. 2, c.

32. See *ST* II–II, q. 83, a. 1.

33. See *ST* II–II, q. 83, a. 1, c.

acknowledges the order God has imposed on the universe. The practical use of reason, in turn, consists in applying one's acquired knowledge to the ordering or commanding of one's own action or of the action of another.

Other persons, whose actions we may want to order, can be our subordinates, our peers, or our superiors. When we are the superior of someone, we order their actions through commands or mandates. When we are ordering the actions of a peer or of a superior, we advise, or we make a petition. A petition is an order of reason addressed to a superior.

Think about the speech of a politician running to become the governor of a state. Voters make the decision of who will obtain this position. In this sense and in accordance with our current politics, voters are the superiors of the candidate.

The speech of the politician is nothing but a natural petition. He thanks his listeners for the attention given to him. He presents to them the reasons why he should be elected. And he formally formulates what he wants them to do, namely, to vote for him.

Note that a petition presupposes a judgment about something to be good. The politician judges that his being the governor is good. But this good is something that is desired and beyond the capacities of the desiring subject. He needs the vote of the people. This good toward which he is oriented is the object of a certain hope.

When we apply this natural structure to Christian prayer, we clearly see that prayer presents to God the object of Christian hope as governed by charity. In prayer, reason is the advocate and interpreter of the desires and hopes of the heart of the Christian.

This is one of the senses in which we interpret what the psalm says, that God hears the desires of the poor (see Ps 9:38). Indeed, their "desire is the cause of their petition, since a petition is like the interpreter of a desire."[34]

In accordance with the natural structure just analyzed, Aquinas identifies four integral elements in prayer as such: prayer, petition, supplication, and thanksgiving. Pay close attention to the following text:

34. *ST* II–II, q. 83, a. 1, ad 1.

Three conditions are requisite for prayer. First, that the person who prays should approach God Whom he prays: this is signified in the word prayer, because *prayer is the raising up of one's mind to God*. The second is that there should be a *petition*, and this is signified in the word intercession. . . . The third condition is the reason for impetrating what we ask for: and this either on the part of God, or on the part of the person who asks. The reason of *impetration* on the part of God is His sanctity, on account of which we ask to be heard. . . . The reason for impetration on the part of the person who asks is *thanksgiving*; since through giving thanks for benefits received we merit to receive yet greater benefits.[35]

Christian prayer, therefore, addresses God as a superior. It gives him thanks, praising or blessing him for his goodness and benefits. It proposes the reasons why he may listen to us. And it asks of the Lord a fitting good, which we desire and hope to obtain through his generosity.

This is the basic configuration or essence of the prayer of blessing, which is binding for every Christian and is done for sinners, enemies, and persecutors.

GOD'S WORSHIP ELEVATED BY THE THEOLOGICAL VIRTUES TO BE CONFIGURED TO CHRIST'S PRAYER

As an act of religion, the prayer of blessing possesses a proper final end. It consists in an order of this same blessing to give the Lord his due as Creator and Ruler of the universe: worship.[36]

As we explained, religion is a human virtue and not a theological virtue because, by itself, it does not immediately unite us with God.[37] Its proper object is the worship of the Lord, not God himself. Yet, because of its great excellence, the virtue of religion

---

35. *ST* II–II, q. 83, a. 17, c; emphasis added.

36. See *ST* II–II, q. 81, a. 1. See also *ST* II–II, q. 81, a. 3.

37. See *ST* II–II, q. 81, a. 5, c.

can command other human virtues, directing their acts to the glory and honor of God.[38]

Religion elevates men who completely submit to the Lord by means of interior and exterior acts, even by means of the offering of external goods.[39] The theological virtues of faith, hope, and charity command and direct the Christian virtue of religion.[40] In this way, the theological virtues provide a superior order to the acts of prayer, connecting the latter with Christ's prayer and with his only sacrifice.

The first act of religion is not prayer but the volitional act of devotion, which consists in a readiness to give oneself completely to the service and worship of God.[41] Devotion is not the same as charity. But charity can augment devotion in an unprecedented manner.[42] It provides a deeper dimension to religion.

In charity, we worship not only the Creator and Ruler, but also our Father and friend. This depth finds its perfection in those moved by the gift of the Holy Spirit of piety.

Devotion moves prayer as an act of religion. It perfects the will in matters pertaining to the worship of God. Thereby, it perfects the moving of the will of other faculties to offer them up to the Lord. True religious prayer has God's glory at its center. Our will moves our intellect to ask God fitting things so that we may worship him. Our supplications help us to acknowledge our poverty and his infinite majesty.[43]

Aquinas presents devotion and prayer, or devoted prayer, as the internal acts of religion which must accompany and animate the exterior acts of adoration, praise, and sacrifice. Adoration worships God with our body while praise worships him with our lips.[44]

---

38. See *ST* II–II, q. 81, a. 1, ad 1. See also *ST* II–II, q. 81, a. 4, ad 1; *ST* II–II, q. 81, a. 6, c.

39. See *ST* II–II, q. 81, a. 7, c and ad 2.

40. See *ST* II–II, q. 81, a. 5, ad 1.

41. See *ST* II–II, q. 82, a. 1, c.

42. *ST* II–II, q. 81, a. 2, ad 1.

43. See *ST* II–II, q. 83, a. 3.

44. Concerning adoration, see *ST* II–II, q. 84, a. 2, c. Concerning praise,

Although God does not need our adoration or praise, public worship manifests the thoughts of those who adore and praise the Lord. In so doing, devotion to and respect for God can grow in men.

Sacrifice is the most synthetic act of religion. As Christians, we have only one sacrifice, the Eucharist, as source and summit of our life. All received graces come from this sacrifice. The whole of our interior and exterior life is ordered to be offered on that same altar.

Consequently, there is an indissoluble connection between the Christian prayer of blessing and Christian sacrifice. All blessings come from Christ and his sacrifice. No blessing can come to us through another way. Obviously, this does not mean that we can bless only during Mass.

BLESSINGS AS SACRAMENTALS

The study of blessings as sacramentals must take place within this broader context of the acts of religion. Blessings as sacramentals have a more restricted meaning. Not every prayer of praise or intercession can count as a sacramental blessing.

Aquinas' theology of sacramentals is in total consonance with our current *Catechism of the Catholic Church*. Blessings have a distinguished place among these sacred signs instituted by the church which are themselves not sacraments.

> Holy Mother Church has, moreover, instituted sacramentals. These are sacred signs which bear a resemblance to the sacraments. They signify effects, particularly of a spiritual nature, which are obtained through the intercession of the Church. By them men are disposed to receive the chief effect of the sacraments, and various occasions in life are rendered holy.[45]

For Thomas, sacramentals are also ordered to remove obstacles for a fruitful reception of the sacraments. They are also a means to

---

see *ST* II–II, q. 91, a. 1, c.

45. *CCC*, 1667.

fight against venial sin: "It is the nature of sacramentals to remit venial sin by such things, like beating the breast and holy water."[46]

For those who are well disposed to their reception, sacramentals are a means to obtain *actual graces*, which make conversion from sin possible. This point was also made explicit by *FS*. Hence, it is important that we see a text from Saint Thomas in this regard.

> Venial sin is forgiven through the fervor of charity, which explicitly or implicitly contains contrition; and so those things that are in themselves of a nature to excite the fervor of charity are said to forgive venial sins. But there are things like that which confer grace, such as are all the sacraments, and things by which impediments to fervor and grace are removed, like holy water, which represses the power of the Enemy, and a bishop's blessing, or even an exercise of humility on our part, like beating the breast, or the Lord's Prayer, and the like.[47]

The *Catechism* explains that every blessing, as a sacramental, is always a form of prayer. This prayer can be accompanied by other signs, such as the sign of the cross.[48] We find here confirmation that sacramental blessings must be understood within the context of the virtue of religion. We can also corroborate that sacramental blessings preserve the natural structure of blessings and prayers previously explained.

Blessings are not diversified according to different species within a genus. Rather, they are kinds or types of prayer, used in different ways in different contexts, by different ministers.

Some blessings belong to the essence of the sacraments as they constitute part of their form. These blessings are always reserved to the proper minister of said sacrament.

Ordained ministers may also celebrate the sacraments using certain sacramental blessings, within the context of the sacraments, but not belonging to the form of the sacrament.

---

46. *In IV Sent.*, d. 17, q. 3, a. 3, qc. 3; emphasis added. See also *ST* III, q. 65, a. 1, ad 6 and 7.

47. *In IV Sent.*, d. 16, q. 2, a. 2, qc. 4. See also *In IV Sent.*, d. 2, q. 1, a. 2, ad 7.

48. See *CCC*, 1668; *Super Mat.*, c. 19, lect. 1, n. 1574.

For instance, the deacon or the priest can bless the baptismal font within the context of the sacrament of baptism. Such blessings do not constitute the essence of the sacrament. Rather, they belong to their solemn celebration.[49]

With respect to the ministers, Christ appears as the blessed one from the Father. Commenting on the Father's words at the Transfiguration, Thomas explains the special way in which Jesus is the beloved and hence the blessed one from the Father.

> Our love is based on a creature's goodness. For a thing is not good because I love it, but rather I love a thing because it is good. But God's love is the cause of goodness in things. And as God poured out goodness in creatures through creation, so in the Son through generation, since he communicates his entire goodness to the Son. Hence creatures are blessed by participation, but he gave the entire goodness to the Son; the Father loves the Son: "and he has given all things into his hand" (John 3:35). Hence Love itself proceeds from the Father loving the Son, and from the Son loving the Father.[50]

In Aquinas' theology, the Lord is the minister of blessings *par excellence*.[51] He himself, as Word, is God's blessing incarnate. Sacraments can confer grace only because they are blessed by Christ[52] and sacramentals are understood in reference to the sacraments.

Hence, Christ, Eternal and High Priest is, *par excellence*, the minister of blessings as well as the very source of every possible blessing which men can receive in the present economy of salvation.

Different blessings are reserved to different ministers, especially blessings of consecration. Thomas teaches that bishops and priests have *potestas* over the Body of Christ in different ways. For

---

49. See *In IV Sent.*, d. 2, q. 1, a. 1, qc. 2, ad 2; *In IV Sent.*, d. 5, q. 2, a. 1, ad qc. 1; *ST* III, q. 66, a. 3, ad 5; *ST* III, q. 66, a. 10, c.

50. *Super Mat.*, c. 17, lect. 1, n. 1436.

51. See *Super Ps. 44*, n. 452.

52. See *ST* III, q. 62, a. 4, ad 3. Christ blesses in a way not possible for the Old Law. See *Super Io.*, c. 5, lect. 2, n. 721.

this reason, certain blessings belong only to bishops while others can also be performed by a priest.

Priests have *potestas* over the sacramental body of Christ. Bishops also have it over the mystical body. Thus, it belongs to the bishop to perform those blessings which determine the place a person occupies in the church as the mystical body of Christ.[53]

Beyond this clarification, Aquinas understands that many blessings are not reserved to the ordained and may be imparted also by lay people in virtue of their baptismal priesthood and the exercise of charity imbedded in the blessing of sinners and enemies.[54]

Nevertheless, Thomas makes an important distinction between the blessings imparted by lay people and those imparted by ordained ministers. The blessings of lay people are connected with their own merits and the holiness of their lives.

The holier the lay person, the more efficacious will his blessing be. Undoubtedly, the merits of saintly lay people are also connected with Christ's merits since the principles of merit in them are merited and dispensed by Jesus.

Yet, the blessing given by an ordained minister is more directly connected with Christ's merits and with the authority of the ordained minister as such. In this case, it is more about the blessing from Christ which arrives to those being blessed through the ministerial instrument.[55]

A FULLER TAXONOMY OF BLESSINGS

After searching for the theology of blessings in the entire *corpus thomisticum*, and in light of all the elements we have already explained, instead of dividing blessings into different species, I think we should consider blessings as a *potential whole* with

---

53. See *In IV Sent.*, d. 13, q. 1, a. 1, qc. 2, ad 2; *In IV Sent.*, d. 24–25.
54. See *CCC*, 1669.
55. See *In IV Sent.*, d. 19, q. 1, a. 2, qc. 1, ad 2; *Super Heb.*, c. 7, lect. 2, n. 343.

different analogous parts. The realm of blessings is similar to the realm of the cardinal virtue of justice, for example.

I am inclined to this option because of the way in which blessings are defined. They are all about saying a good which tends to *foster* it. Different blessings foster the good in various *degrees*. Consequently, the very definition of blessing seems to be fulfilled in different degrees of perfection in the different blessings.

In light of this principle, we can offer now a fuller taxonomy of blessings. This taxonomy is also important for the moral theology of blessings, because it underscores the first analogate within the series, namely, that blessing in which all the rest participates.

The first analogate, where the definition of blessing is most perfectly found, corresponds to God's blessing. God's Word is infallible in its blessing. He immediately causes the good that he says. It is a perfect imperative blessing.

The second place, within the order found in imperative blessings, corresponds to the imperative blessings of Christ, Eternal High Priest. He is capable of blessing the sacraments themselves, instituting them.

The third place, always within imperative blessings, would correspond to the blessing imparted by Christ's ordained ministers, capable of celebrating the sacraments and of instituting sacramentals and blessings through them.

The fourth place in this same order of imperative blessings corresponds to the lay person who performs a sacramental by virtue of his baptismal priesthood. However, this is not the place to evaluate the different modes of efficaciousness of these blessings.

After imperative blessings, we have the realm of subjunctive or desiderative blessings. This kind of blessing is the one proper to the Christian prayer of intercession in general. When it fulfills all its requirements and it rightly asks for things needed for salvation, this prayer is infallible in its petition. Lastly, we would have indicative blessings which foster the good by acknowledging it is already in existence.

The taxonomy here presented is not meant to be exclusive. There are other possible divisions, not made by essential criterions, which may be very useful. For example, sometimes we distinguish sins thanks to non-essential criteria. Thus, we consider sins of thought, words, and deeds.

Similarly, we could speak of more or less formal blessings, within a given liturgical context in the Church or more spontaneous, or those having, as their recipients, people in more need of God's mercy and further away from Christ's teachings, etc. These are accidental divisions. But these distinctions are very useful, especially when they are based on the degree of their solemnity, with an eye open to the circumstances, which assist in the avoidance of scandal. We will come back to this topic in our last chapter.

BLASPHEMY, SACRILEGE, AND BLESSINGS

The words freely used by the ordained minister in the blessing, as well as his intention, must be consonant with the charity of Christ's heart. Adopting the perspective of religion, Jesus' own prayer, including his prayer for his enemies and persecutors, must be the canon and rule for the blessings imparted by his ordained ministers. Following his own example, we should make our own the title of this book: bless and do not curse them!

At the cross, we find the greatest display of charity in the human will of Christ. Firstly, he is loving God above all things. This is the most important commandment of the law (see Matt 22:36–40). In the second place, he is also loving all of us sinners, his enemies (see Rom 5:10). He is doing so in God, for God, and because of God.

That charity in his affect or intention is effectively and exteriorly expressed in acts of religion. Most importantly, this faithful expression takes place in Christ's sacrifice to the Father and in a vocal and exterior prayer which asks for the blessing of mercy: "Father, forgive them, because they do not know what they are doing" (Luke 23:24).

If we follow this example, in which words faithfully express charity, we will not fall into the disorders of blasphemy or sacrilege.

It is important to explain how to avoid these sins against religion because *FS* has been accused by its detractors of fostering them.

Given its contrariety to faith, the reader may be surprised to find blasphemy in this context of religion. Blasphemy is a verbal infidelity that is *uttered*. It is a way of speaking that offends God. It opposes not only faith but also the confession of that same faith. And the latter is intimately connected with religion and the public worship due to God.[56]

Thomas explains about the blasphemous character of the blessing given by a sinful priest: "the blessing of a sinful priest, inasmuch as he acts unworthily is deserving of a curse, and is reputed an infamy and a blasphemy, and not a prayer."[57]

The Lord is goodness itself. He deserves to be acknowledged, loved, and blessed. The confession of faith presupposes that one has living faith. It is a faith animated by charity and moved by the latter to its public manifestation.

Therefore, who falls into the sin of blasphemy? Aquinas answers "whoever either denies anything befitting God, or affirms anything unbefitting Him, [because he] disparages the Divine goodness."[58]

Thomas continues to explain that blasphemy can happen in two ways. It may happen "merely in respect of the opinion in the intellect."[59] But it can also happen that this opinion is accompanied by "a certain detestation in the affections."[60]

The Angelic Doctor uses as a reverse example how faith is informed by charity. Analogously, this opinion that disparages the divine goodness may be accompanied or informed by an affective detestation:

> Accordingly, this disparagement of the Divine goodness
> is either in the intellect alone, or in the affections also. If
> it is in thought only, it is blasphemy of the heart, whereas

56. See *ST* II–II, q. 13, a. 1.
57. *ST* III, q. 82, a. 5, ad 3.
58. *ST* II–II, q. 13, a. 1, c.
59. *ST* II–II, q. 13, a. 1, c.
60. *ST* II–II, q. 13, a. 1, c.

if it betrays itself outwardly in speech it is blasphemy of the tongue. It is in this sense that blasphemy is opposed to confession of faith.[61]

A more perfect blasphemy requires the deliberated opposition of the will to divine honor.[62] Blasphemies can occur in affirmations and in negations. They can be directed immediately against God or they can be directed against him through the mediation of an insult to the saints or to any of the Lord's good works in his creatures.[63]

How could a blessing be blasphemous? As a sacramental, a blessing praises the Lord and petitions a good as coming from him. To call evil good, or to ask as if it were good, something that is really evil would make the blessing blasphemous.

The same thing would happen if we said that something is evil, when in reality it is good. Remember the example of cursing the devil as a creature of God. That would be a blasphemy like it would be to curse a sinner without distinguishing his guilt from his own created good nature.

To say that a work of God as such is evil is also a way of blaspheming against him. If someone were to curse a person, who actively practices homosexual behavior or extramarital sex in general, without these distinctions, would actually incur a serious sin.

Blasphemy is a mortal sin *ex genere suo*. It is an act opposed, not only to the confession of faith and to religion, but also to charity itself.[64] In a certain sense (*secundum quid*), Thomas teaches that it is the gravest of sins, especially if we consider the measure in which it aggravates *infidelitas*, infidelity, also translated as unfaithfulness, or unbelief.

> Blasphemy is opposed to the confession of faith, so that
> it contains the gravity of unbelief [*infidelitatis*]: while the
> sin is aggravated if the will's detestation is added thereto,

---

61. *ST* II–II, q. 13, a. 1, c.
62. See *ST* II–II, q. 13, a. 1, ad 1.
63. See *ST* II–II, q. 13, a. 1, ad 2 and 3.
64. See *ST* II–II, q. 13, a. 2, c.

and yet more, if it breaks out into words, even as love and confession add to the praise of faith. Therefore, since, as stated above, unbelief [*infidelitas*] is the greatest of sins in respect of its genus, it follows that blasphemy also is a very great sin, through belonging to the same genus as unbelief and being an aggravated form of that sin.[65]

Even if this is a *secundum quid*, this theological precision helps to not diminish the importance of the use of words in blessings. Blasphemous blessings or curses are serious sins. They should not be taken lightly.

The permission to bless persons in sinful unions granted by *FS* is not necessarily the permission to a blasphemous blessing, provided we fulfill the requirements already mentioned.

He who blesses must love the same things Christ's heart loves in those persons. He must also ask for them the same things Christ wants to give to them. This blessing could become blasphemous if it would call good the sin of these people or if it would ask for something that fosters sin and not their conversion.

Yet, the sheer presence of two sinners, who ask for a blessing, even if these sinners are allied in that sin, does not impose a necessity on the priest or deacon giving the blessing to approve their sin or the necessity to will for them the prosperity of their evil acts.

The presence of these sinners is not the fundamental element that constitutes the moral species of the act of blessing. The *words* used in the blessing and the *end* in the will of the one using those words are the definitive factors. Other circumstances should also be considered but we will come back to that.

The words must be true, calling good what is good and evil what is evil. The intention of the end must be in consonance with the love of Christ's heart. As the adagio goes, *bonum ex integra causa, malum ex quocumque defectu*. Provided the right circumstances, at least avoiding the circumstantial dangers *FS* explains, so long as these two elements (object and intention) are there, there is no reason to call such a blessing blasphemous.

---

65. *ST* II–II, q. 13, a. 3, c.

As sacred signs and sacramentals, blessings are oriented to the proper end of religion, namely, the worship of God. This orientation makes blessings worthy of respect and reverence.

Although holiness consists in the perfection of charity, and properly speaking, as holiness is found only in personal beings, we also speak of sacred or holy things, because of their orientation to God's worship. There is a special sin when one disrespects sacred things: "Whatever pertains to irreverence for sacred things is an injury to God, and comes under the head of sacrilege."[66]

Every blasphemous blessing is also sacrilegious. But we could have a non-blasphemous blessing that is sacrilegious, for instance, if the end of the blessing would not be the worship of God but some personal gain of the one offering the blessing like money, fame, prestige, the approval of others, being fashionable or famous, etc.

Sacred things are to be used for the worship of God. They must not be subordinated to other ends, like giving importance to oneself, or acquiring preeminence over others. Such subordinations constitute an irreverence.

The blessing of couples in irregular unions could be sacrilegious if the minister uses these blessings irreverently. But there is nothing in these blessings that makes them necessarily sacrilegious. They could be. But they could not be as well. The whole question would fall more, not on the people being blessed, but rather on the evil intention of the minister in the use of the blessing.

Human words have the capacity of expressing what it is that is acknowledged as good and under which aspect this acknowledgement is made. They can also express what it is for which one is thankful to God or what is praised because of him. And they can certainly express what it is that one asks for these persons of the Lord.

Hence, these words are the decisive factor. One should not judge the morality of these blessings simply on the sheer fact that these persons present themselves together to be blessed. The fact that they are sinners, that one commits a given sin, that he or she

66. *ST* II–II, q. 99, a. 1, c.

cooperates in the sin of another, are not the essential factors which determine the goodness of the blessing.

Imagine the following hypothetical situation. A given country is undergoing a civil war. One of the sides persecutes the Catholic Church. A battalion from this anti-Catholic side captures a bishop. They condemn him to be killed by a firing squad.

This bishop is now before his executioners. The moment of his death is imminent. Yet, this holy bishop looks at them and loves them with the love of Christ's heart. His last act, as they fire, is to bless them, praying in a loud voice for their conversion and salvation: "Father, forgive and bless these men, grant them the gift of conversion and salvation." As he says these words, he makes the sign of the cross over the firing squad.

No one would have the courage to say that this bishop is in hell because his last act on this earth was a mortal sin. No one would say that he was imparting a blasphemous, sacrilegious, and scandalous blessing, which approves the horrendous act for which these other men were gathered, namely, the killing of an innocent man.

Yet, note that this bishop is blessing these men as they are committing this grave sin. It is not a past sin. It is taking place at that very moment. The reason these men in the firing squad are there as a group is precisely to murder him. That is what makes them a firing squad. The bishop does not make many signs of the cross, only one to the whole group. But no one concludes that the bishop sins mortally. His *words* are the key!

We all understand that this is a case of a martyr who manifests with his last words and gestures the living image of Christ, Good Shepherd and Eternal High Priest. Like the Lord, he is loving God above all things. He is also loving his executioners in God, because of God, and for God. His blessing is an act of religion, a faithful effective expression of this affective disposition which conforms to Christ's charity for his enemies on the cross.

SIMONY AND BLESSINGS

The last deformation we are going to examine is that of simony. This sin deals with the deliberate choice of selling and buying sacred spiritual things.[67] Aquinas considers this sin extremely grave.

If an adult in danger of death has as his only option to receive baptism from the hands of simoniac priest, Thomas argues that it is better not to receive such baptism and to trust in the baptism of desire.

> If it were an adult in danger of death that wished to be baptized, and the priest were unwilling to baptize him without being paid, he ought, if possible, to be baptized by someone else. And if he is unable to have recourse to another, he must by no means pay a price for Baptism, and should rather die without being baptized, because for him the baptism of desire would supply the lack of the sacrament.[68]

Note that the selling and buying inherent in simony is not only about money. It can also be about other things which have an economic value.[69] The retribution received could also be some service or favor, some social prestige accompanied by certain privileges, some fame, or verbal approval.

Blessings could be the object of selling and buying in different ways. The will to sell and to buy must be deliberate. Such deliberate will may be absent in the case of a hypocrite who does something spiritual to gain the praises of others but does so in a furtive manner. In this case, we are not dealing, strictly speaking, with selling and buying but rather with the stealing or robbery of those praises.[70]

The blessings allowed by *FS* are not necessarily a case of simony. They could be so or not. Those who celebrate the alleged doctrinal discontinuity of the document, and moved by worldly

---

67. *ST* II–II, q. 100, a. 1, c.
68. *ST* II–II, q. 100, a. 2, ad 1.
69. See *ST* II–II, q. 100, a. 5, c.
70. See *ST* II–II, q. 100, a. 5, ad 4.

motivations, perform blessings forbidden by the document itself ruthlessly to gain notoriety, put their own salvation at risk. They resemble those in the *Letter to the Romans*, who, through sweet words and blessings and for their own personal gain, seduce the hearts of innocent persons.[71]

71. See *Super Rom.*, c. 16, lect. 2, n. 1214–16.

4

Blessings and Prudence

THIS LAST CHAPTER BRINGS us to the way in which blessings must be informed by acquired and infused prudence, animated in turn by charity. As part of the moral theology of blessings, we will study now the nominal definition of prudence and its essence as right reason about action (*recta ratio agibilium*) in connection with what we call discernment, the way in which it is the mother and custodian of the virtues, how all virtues are prudent, the importance of circumstances and circumspection, and how prudence is the key to avoid scandal in giving blessings to people in irregular unions.

NOMINAL DEFINITION OF PRUDENCE

Once again, we must begin with the nominal definition of prudence. The English word "prudence," comes from the Latin noun "*prudentia*" and from the Greek nouns πρόνοια, φρόνησις, and διάκρισις.

The Latin noun already echoes the noun "providence" (*providentia*).[1] What stands out from the Latin names is that to be prudent is to be able to provide for oneself or for others. It consists

1. See Ramírez, *Prudencia*, 16.

in being able to foresee with one's mind (*pro-videre*), to see far ahead (*porro videns*).

The Greek origins of our virtue, in turn, are richer. They give us more nuances about the kind of providence which prudence is all about.

The noun πρόνοια is usually rendered in Latin as *providentia*. The reason behind this common translation is that πρόνοια corresponds to the English verbs "to for-see," "to see ahead," or "to have an anticipated knowledge." The English word "prognosis," for instance, finds its root here. This etymology emphasizes how prudence is a kind of knowledge about the future, grounded in the memory of the past, and in the understanding of the present.[2]

Thomas teaches that this knowledge of the future "is the chief part of prudence, to which two other parts are directed—namely, remembrance of the past, and understanding of the present; inasmuch as from the remembrance of what is past and the understanding of what is present, we gather how to provide for the future."[3]

The noun φρόνησις is usually translated into Latin as "*prudentia*." It literally means a firm thought ordered to obtain something good and to avoid something evil.[4] There is a sense of *protection* included in this term. The English word "diaphragm" comes from this same root. And, as is known, the diaphragm *protects* the heart.

The Greek word φρήν came to mean the heart as the center of our soul, as the synergy of our thoughts and feelings. This etymology already hints at the fact that prudence is a custodian, a protector of the most intimate and core element in the human person: the center of the soul, that is, the intellect and the will in their reciprocal immanence.

Along this same line, Aristotle noticed a connection between the etymologies of prudence (φρόνησις) and temperance (σωφροσύνη). Thomas explains that "because prudence is concerned with good and bad things to be done, for this reason temperance

2. See *In III Sent.*, d. 33, q. 3, a. 1, qc. 1.

3. *ST* I, q. 22, a. 1, c.

4. See Ramírez, *Prudencia*, 19.

is called in Greek *sophrosyne* (as it were, a thing preserving the reason) from which prudence gets the name phronesis."[5]

This etymological connection also serves to point out that prudence is a virtue, which presupposes the moral virtues, especially those in the realm of temperance. The latter preserve reason. They do it in different ways. But we are now interested in one of them.

Prudence is right reason in acting (*recta ratio agibilium*). It identifies and commands the right means to attain our due end. However, for prudence to identify these means, we need to be *already inclined* to our due end.

Part of this inclination is given by nature. The first principles of the natural law in the intellect (*synderesis*) have a corresponding inclination in the will. However, these inclinations are not enough. They are too universal. We also need to rectify our appetites by growing in the moral virtues.

The noun "διάκρισις" is often translated as "discernment" or "discretion." It presupposes freedom of choice. It refers to the personal and mental activity of distinguishing in each set of circumstances what is truly good or best. This noun is used by very prominent and authoritative authors, such as John Cassian, in the rule of Saint Benedict, Saint Gregory the Great, Saint Bernard, and Richard of Saint Victor.

The noun "διάκρισις" adds something important to our initial understanding of prudence. Discernment is about discriminating between good and evil. But it is also about discriminating or making a right judgment about what is *best* in each situation. In other words, prudence is not only about good and evil, but also about competing goods, too!

The Fathers of the Desert spoke of prudence as διάκρισις with the image of the lamp that enlightens our footsteps in our spiritual life (see Ps 119:105). To understand prudence as a discerning light, it is important to realize that once upon a time, there was no electricity. To walk at night was very dangerous. A lamp was needed. It allowed one to see the territory needed to walk few steps ahead.

5. *In VI Ethic.*, lect. 4, n. 1169.

A lamp does not light the whole way at once. It shows the way in the near future. Prudence as discernment acts in the same way. It shows the steps along the way, the right means, which are conducive to the final end of the human person.

Some contemporary authors would make a very sharp distinction between prudence (φρόνησις) and discernment (διάκρισις), as if they were two different realities. Thomas, instead, would consider them synonymous: "Prudence is merely a certain rectitude of discretion in any actions or matters whatever."[6]

Ramírez explains well why this identification between prudence and discernment is so clear for Aquinas:

> Thomas read daily Cassian's conferences. He perfectly knew the rule of Saint Benedict since his stay at Monte Cassino. Looking at the frequency with which he referred to them, Thomas displayed a great mastery over the works of Saint Gregory, Saint Bernard, and Richard of Saint Victor. Aquinas collected all their tradition concerning διάκρισις and inserted in his own treatise on prudence, even if he uses the word discernment only once in that same treatise.[7]

This scholarly note from Father Ramírez is extremely valuable. Teaching discernment is the same as teaching a great part of prudence.

Spiritual direction should never be foreign to our formation in this virtue. Prudence as discernment is needed to be perfect: "For a person is perfect, when he discerns between good and evil, between good and better, and between evil and worse."[8]

---

6. *ST* I–II, q. 65, a. 1, c.

7. Ramírez, *Prudencia*, 30. The reference is *ST* II–II, q. 47, a. 1, ad 1. Yet, Aquinas has many texts in which he uses prudence and discernment as synonymous. Outside of the *Summa*, one could read, for instance, *In III Sent.*, d. 33, q. 2, a. 5, c and ad 2; *In III Sent.*, d. 36, a. 1, c; *De Virtutibus*, a. 2; *In VI Ethic.*, lect. 11, n. 1279, *In III De anima*, lect. 14, n. 796, etc. Thomas identifies prudence and discernment within the *Summa*, outside the so-called treatise on prudence. For instance, one can read *ST* II–II, q. 188, a. 6, c and ad 3.

8. *Super Heb.*, c. 5, lect. 2, n. 274. See also *ST* II–II, q. 47, a. 1, ad 1.

This is a great point of contact between Aquinas and other great masters of discernment such as Saint Ignatius of Loyola or the Fathers of the Desert.[9] The latter, for instance, adopted this word (διάκρισις) to speak about prudence as discernment or knowledge, which unveils the attacks of the enemy of our soul.

Prudence adds something very important to discernment. Remember the chart with the process of human action. Properly speaking, discernment belongs to the process of counsel and judgment. Prudence, instead, includes discernment but is richer. Prudence includes choice, and, above all, command and execution. Discernment does not.

MOTHER AND CUSTODIAN

Saint Anthony Abbot considered prudence to be the greatest among the cardinal virtues. He called it the mother, the custodian, and the moderator of the moral virtues.[10] Aquinas knows this tradition well and reports it in his own explanation on the value of prudence.

> Prudence is the more principal of the cardinal virtues, and to it all the others are traced back as to a cause. Whence Anthony says that the *discernment that pertains to prudence* is the mother, custodian, and moderator of the virtues.[11]

Discretion or discernment *belongs* to prudence. It must correspond to one or to several of its acts. In general, prudence deals with the intellectual acts that we have mentioned before, when we studied in our first chapter commands and desires and mediated subjects of truth, namely, those acts of counsel, judgment, and command.

---

9. For a great explanation of discernment in the tradition of Saint Ignatius of Loyola, see Gallagher, *Discernment of Spirits*.

10. See Turonensis, *Vitae Patrum*, Bk. 4, c. 42; Cassianus, *Collationum*, Bk. 2, c. 2.

11. *In III Sent.*, d. 33, q. 2, a. 5, c; emphasis added.

Discernment is easily associated with the first one, with counsel as perfected by faith and by the gift of the Holy Spirit with that same name. It also belongs to judgment, in which case one has multiple good possible choices to choose from.

Prudence is the mother, custodian, and moderator of the moral virtues because it perfects reason, and it helps in regulating the means to the ends of the other virtues.

Virtues move through inclination. Now, "every inclination of a nature demands a certain cognition that both pre-establishes the end, inclines one to the end, and provides the things by which one attains the end."[12]

There are certain evident principles of the moral life. Good is to be done. Evil is to be avoided. Human persons should act in accordance with reason. One should not allow one's passions to rule his life unless they are moderated and informed by right reason. One should treat others the way he ought to be treated, etc.

The knowledge of these principles and others like them is habitually contained in an intellectual habit called "synderesis." They do not contain explicitly all the acts of the virtues. However, they contain them in general terms as the ones just mentioned. We refer to these principles as the "natural law."[13]

Aquinas also refers to this habit by using the expression "natural reason." Such a knowledge takes care of pre-establishing the end. The knowledge of these principles presupposes the knowledge of goods which are *evidently* linked to our happiness. Such knowledge with evidence, such natural knowledge, triggers natural inclinations of the will. And these inclinations are part of what Thomas calls the "will as nature" (*voluntas ut natura*). They correspond to that simple volition identified in the chart offered in our first chapter.[14]

But prudence is not to be confused with this natural knowledge. Prudence and synderesis are different habits. But they

---

12. *In III Sent.*, d. 33, q. 2, a. 5, c.

13. See *ST* I–II, q. 94, a. 3, c. See Brock, *Light*. See also Rhonheimer, *Natural Law*.

14. See *ST* I–II, q. 94, a. 2, c.

go together. Prudence perfects reason to provide the things that are for the end, that lead to its attainment, those things which in common parlance we call "the means" and that Aquinas calls *ea quae sunt ad finem*.

For example, prudence establishes how many alcoholic drinks a person should have, in a given day and in accordance with what he has eaten, to act in accordance with the virtue of sobriety.

Prudence does not appoint the end to the moral virtues. It does not appoint the end of drinking moderately in accordance with reason. Synderesis already prescribed in general that one should act in this way. Prudence regulates the means to achieve this goal.[15] This regulation is of the utmost importance.

In the case of the acquired virtues, prudence is the *mother of the virtues*, because "through right reason there is an inclination to their proper end, which inclination is the intention of the end in the acquired virtues insofar as, due to actions regulated by reason, the habit of the virtue causing this inclination is brought about."[16]

When I have repeatedly and intensely acted with gratitude or chastity, I experience an inclination to their particular ends. This inclination is key to growing in these virtues. Prudence has engendered said inclination as its mother by establishing the mean of virtue in these particular actions, which I repeatedly and intensely performed. In this sense, prudence generated these inclinations, which will mature into acquired virtues. For this reason, it can be said to be their mother.

Prudence is said to be the custodian and moderator because it discerns what is harmful or helpful in the attainment of the end of each virtue. Prudence "makes straight the path of each virtue that stretches to its end, insofar as, through deliberation and choice, useful things are separated out from harmful, relative to the end of the virtue."[17]

The discernment which belongs to prudence perfects that process of deliberation and choice by empowering the intellectual

15. See *In III Sent.*, d. 33, q. 2, a. 5, c.

16. *In III Sent.*, d. 33, q. 2, a. 5, c.

17. *In III Sent.*, d. 33, q. 2, a. 5, c.

acts of counsel and judgment. Through these acts, one can see, as it were, the obstacles and the deviations in the path of a given virtue due to the vast number of circumstances we find in particular and concrete actions. Prudence discerns and commands what to do in order to attain the due goal. And it does so, not autonomously and independently from God and his providence, but in collaboration with it.

ALL VIRTUES ARE PRUDENT

As we have seen, prudence is the mold and mother of all the moral virtues. It is their measure. The Ten Commandments pertain to the execution of prudence. *Omnis virtus moralis debet esse prudens.* All virtue is necessarily prudent. Even our good innate inclinations are not true virtues, unless they are regulated by prudence. Sometimes we call them "*natural* virtues." But this is a very broad and imprecise use of the term.[18]

Saint Ambrose explains the role of prudence as the source of moral obligation and as the condition for the existence of other virtues: "The first source of duty, then, is prudence. For what is more of a duty than to give to the Creator all one's devotion and reverence? This source, however, is drawn off into other virtues. For justice cannot exist without prudence, since it demands no small amount of prudence to see whether a thing is just or unjust."[19]

The Saint from Milan continues distinguishing the performance of good deeds from the virtues. Some men perform just deeds without being just: "they do deeds decreed by law but either unwillingly or because of ignorance or for some other reason like gain, and not out of love for the very works of justice."[20]

To have a virtue, one must be prudent. Moral virtue rectifies the intention of the end. "But the things designed by nature to be done for the end do not pertain to moral virtue, but to some other

18. See George, "Aquinas on the Dangers of Natural Virtue."
19. *De Officiis*, I, 27.
20. *In VI Ethic.*, lect. 10, n. 1271.

power, that is, to a certain other operative principle that discovers ways leading to ends. So, a principle of this kind [prudence] is necessary in order that a man be virtuous."[21] Prudence is a specific virtue distinct from other virtues, even if all human virtues participate in prudence, as we have already explained, and the latter is included in their very definition.[22]

CIRCUMSPECTION

Circumspection makes a reference to the capacity to compare the means with the circumstances. Circumspection is different from foresight as providence insofar as the latter looks at what is suitable for an end according to its nature, while circumspection considers if something is suitable for the end, not because of its nature, but because of its circumstances.[23]

Circumstances have a very peculiar status in the theory of moral action. Let us compare human actions with a natural substance, like a horse. The color of the horse is an accident to its substance. Similarly, a circumstance is that which stands around the substance of the action, as its accident.

Yet, there is a peculiar difference in this comparison. The color of the horse is not part of its essence and cannot change the essence or the nature of the horse. However, in the case of human actions, circumstances have the capacity to alter the very substance or essence of the action.

An act of theft could be transformed into one of sacrilege, given the appropriate circumstances, if the theft, for example, is a consecrated chalice from a church. The consummation of marriage by two newlyweds can be totally transformed from a good moral action to an evil one, if the wrong time and place are chosen.

Circumspection is quite important in the execution of prudent actions. One needs the capacity to compare the means with

---

21. *In VI Ethic.*, lect. 10, n. 1271.
22. See *In II Ethic.*, lect. 7, n. 323; *In III Sent.*, d. 33, q. 1, a. 1, qc. 2, ad 1.
23. See *ST* II–II, q. 49, a. 7, ad 3.

the circumstances. Otherwise, he may not direct the means rightly to the end. This point will be crucial to impart blessings appropriately, having charity toward those being blessed and choosing, not only the right truthful words, but also the right time, place, manner, tone, etc.

It is not enough that the end in question is good. The means must be good as well: "It belongs to prudence chiefly to direct something aright to an end; and this is not done aright unless both the end be good, and the means good and suitable."[24]

For the means to be good, one needs to compare them with the changing circumstances. The latter vary a lot. There can be a great variety of combinations in them.

However, *de facto*, there is a limited number to be considered: "Though the number of possible circumstances be infinite, the number of actual circumstances is not; and the judgment of reason in matters of action is influenced by things which are few in number."[25]

Since circumstances can affect the very substance of the morality of our actions, it is very important to have circumspection to be prudent. Indeed, it may happen "that a thing is good in itself and suitable to the end, and nevertheless becomes evil or unsuitable to the end, by reason of some combination of circumstances."[26] This teaching can also be applied to the imparting of blessings. The time, the place, the vestments, the context of the whole blessing, and many other factors must be considered.

In this sense, prudence fixes the circumstances of good moral actions which engender virtues: "Circumstances are the concern of prudence, because prudence has to fix them [*sicut ad determinandum eas*]."[27]

Prudence determines or fixes those circumstances, and that very action collaborates in the formation of the moral virtues because "on the other hand, they [circumstances] are the concern of

---

24. *ST* II–II, q. 49, a. 7, c.
25. *ST* II–II, q. 49, a. 7, ad 1.
26. *ST* II–II, q. 49, a. 7, c.
27. *ST* II–II, q. 49, a. 7, ad 2.

moral virtues, insofar as moral virtues are perfected by the fixing of circumstances."[28]

The consideration about circumspection and the capacity circumstances have to impact the very nature of moral actions show how prudence is also needed to avoid sins treated before, such as blasphemy, sacrilege, or simony. It is not possible to consider them all. In fact, the purpose of this book is not a casuistry of blessings but a true and proper moral theology of them.

CIRCUMSTANCES AND SCANDAL

The brief explanations we have offered thus far are meant to alert the reader to the fact that the pastoral use of blessings promoted by *FS* is not only connected with truth, charity, and religion, but also with prudence, especially with the role this last virtue plays in avoiding the real danger of scandal.[29]

As we already said, *ex genere suo*, blessings are a morally good act. Furthermore, Christian blessings are a matter of divine precept. We are commanded by the Lord to bless others. Yet, for the particular act of blessing another to be morally good, it is not enough that this act contains the right form in its words and that it is rightly ordered to the ends of religion and charity. It must also have its due commensuration to right circumstances. Without this due commensuration, the act may be morally evil. Prudence plays an indispensable role in this matter.

Once again, Aquinas can shed some clarity on this problem by explaining what exactly scandal is:

> While going along the spiritual way, a man may be disposed to a spiritual downfall by another's word or deed, in so far, to wit, as one man by his injunction, inducement or example, moves another to sin; and this is scandal properly so called. Now, nothing by its very nature disposes a man to spiritual downfall, except that which has some lack of rectitude, since what is perfectly right,

28. *ST* II–II, q. 49, a. 7, ad 2.

29. See Perez-Lopez and Perez-Lopez, "Catholic Conscience."

secures man against a fall, instead of conducing to his downfall. Scandal is, therefore, fittingly defined as *something less rightly done or said, that occasions another's spiritual downfall.*[30]

Blessings could be defective. They could be so in their form or in their order to God's glory and the salvation of souls. In these cases, they can also be a cause of scandal. The deformation and disorder of a moral act count as lack of rectitude. If the blessing is neither deformed nor disordered, but is not commeasured to its due circumstances, we still have a lack of rectitude which can cause another's spiritual downfall.

For this reason, *FS* explains that the blessings given to people in irregular unions must be carried out in a particular manner and taking certain precautions. They must avoid any semblance of approval of sin. They must avoid any semblance of equating those unions to marriage. These blessings cannot be solemn and public.

FS does not account for all the possible circumstances. *No document can do that.* The prudence of the ordained minister cannot be substituted by casuistry. It can be aided, however, by the clarity we seek from Aquinas in this book, concerning his moral theology of blessings.

It is very fitting that *FS* does not want to create fixed rituals to bless persons in these complicated situations. The variety of circumstances in which these persons may live is vast. Consider a few examples.

A given blessing may be very appropriate for a divorced person and remarried civilly, who lives chastely in that second union. But another form of the blessing may be more appropriate for the couple not ready yet to live in complete continence.

The choice of words may vary significantly in one case and in the other. Such a choice of words is an exercise of the virtue of pastoral prudence. It is made in view of the different circumstances, and it aims at manifesting, in a simple and clear manner, the charity of Christ's heart for these persons.

---

30. *ST* II–II, q. 43, a. 1, c; emphasis added.

The consideration of the circumstances is extremely important. But there is no reason to forbid *a priori*, as something intrinsically evil always and everywhere (*semper et pro semper*), the blessing of two persons who are cooperating in evil. The example of the execution of the bishop mentioned before shows that clearly, because of the choice of his words and the intention of his heart, and because there is no way that such an act causes scandal in other persons.

Aquinas distinguishes between passive and active scandal. Active scandal is in the person who commits a public sin, thereby inducing others to sin. It can also be present in the person who, lacking prudence, commits a merely apparent sin, which has the same effect of leading others to sin.

In turn, passive scandal is in the person who suffers it. It can take place when a truly good action of someone, an action vested with all its right circumstances, becomes an occasion of sin for a person because this last one is ill-disposed.

In this case, the person who performs the good action is not the cause of sin. It is the person scandalized who takes as an occasion to sin something that lacks nothing for its rectitude.[31]

This scandalized person does this because he or she already suffers from a certain spiritual ruin, a certain ignorance, weakness, or malice.[32] Spiritual goods are not to be abandoned because the wicked are scandalized by it. The Pharisees were scandalized in this manner because of Christ's teachings.

The cases of the weak and of the ignorant present a different scenario. The possibility of their scandal should not be the reason why spiritual goods needed for salvation are abandoned. But if these goods are not those needed for salvation, prudence may differ in action until the scandal is avoided by giving proper instruction or by providing comfort.[33]

It is perfectly understandable that in certain cultural contexts, in Africa for example, the pastoral use of blessings for persons in

31. See *ST* II–II, q. 43, a. 1, ad 4.
32. See *ST* II–II, q. 43, a. 2, c and a. 7, c.
33. See *ST* II–II, q. 43, a. 7, c.

irregular unions may be a cause of scandal. The reason why these people may be disposed to be scandalized may not be malice.

The blessings in question are not like baptism, a good that is needed for salvation. Hence, it is possible to postpone the implementation of the document. The goal of this deferral, however, must be a greater instruction of the faithful concerning the Catholic teaching on blessings.

In no way should this be interpreted as if what is valid for one culture is not valid for another. Truth is always valid. It is eternal. As Catholics, we are not cultural relativists.[34] Culture cannot be the measure of truth.

In fact, Jesus who is Truth is the measure of every culture (see John 14:6). The Lord commanded us to bless and not to curse. Such a commandment comes from him. It is true and always valid. It measures every culture, including that of Africa.

---

34. See Perez-Lopez, "Educación y relativismo." See also Perez-Lopez, *Enseñar a amar.*

Conclusion

In this book, we have offered the main coordinates of Aquinas' moral theology of blessings, understanding their nature and their connection with the virtues of veracity, charity, religion and prudence. Our examination of Aquinas' moral theology of blessings leads us to conclude that the object of Christian blessings is coextensive with the object of charity. This is the most important light in order to understand the divine command to bless and not curse.

Although we have not presented in the book an analysis of the text of *FS*, the attentive reader will easily infer that Aquinas' moral theology of blessings provides a way of interpreting *FS* that accomplishes different goals. It avoids a rushed judgment on the document based on ideological prejudices. It shuns the hermeneutics of suspicion toward the magisterium. And it also avoids either the celebrating or the lamenting of an alleged rupture between this declaration and previous moral teachings.

The theology of the Angelic Doctor explains why some of the public blessings of homosexual couples we have witnessed in the media are indeed blasphemous, sacrilegious, and scandalous. They must be avoided. They should never be called pastoral because they are contrary to Christ's pastoral charity.

Moreover, Thomas' theology also exposes the error of thinking that blessing *couples* in these irregular unions is something wrong always and everywhere (*semper et pro semper*). It even dispels the belief that scandal will *never* be avoided if this document is implemented.

Cardinal Ladaria's response to the dubium on March 15, 2023 is not in contradiction with *FS*. Ladaria's response is a definitive "no" to the blessing of sin. Cardinal Fernandez' declaration also says that sin can never be blessed. It is in continuity with the response from Ladaria. But Cardinal Fernandez expands on the possibility of blessing sinners. In this sense, it constitutes a certain pastoral novelty, a pastoral *novum*.

In light of this book, we can surely conclude that this novelty is not a doctrinal novelty with respect to Aquinas' moral theology of blessings. The latter is larger and richer. Rather, in *FS*, we have a development of the pastoral possibility of blessing sinners, briefly mentioned in Cardinal Ladaria's response.[1]

Consider this key section of *FS*:

> Within the horizon outlined here appears the possibility of blessings for couples in irregular situations and for couples of the same sex, the form of which should not be fixed ritually by ecclesial authorities to avoid producing confusion with the blessing proper to the Sacrament of Marriage. In such cases, a blessing may be imparted that not only has an ascending value but also involves the invocation of a blessing that descends from God upon those who—recognizing themselves to be destitute and in need of his help—*do not claim a legitimation of their own status, but who beg that all that is true, good, and humanly valid in their lives and their relationships be enriched, healed, and elevated by the presence of the Holy Spirit.* These forms of blessing express a supplication that God may grant those aids that come from the impulses of his Spirit—what classical theology calls "*actual grace*"—so that human relationships may mature and grow in *fidelity to the Gospel,* that they may be *freed from their imperfections* and frailties, and that they may

---

1. "The answer to the proposed *dubium* does not preclude the blessings given to individual persons with homosexual inclinations, who manifest the will to live in fidelity to the revealed plans of God as proposed by Church teaching. Rather, it declares illicit any form of blessing that tends to acknowledge their unions as such." *Responsum* of the Congregation for the Doctrine of the Faith to a *dubium* regarding the blessing of the unions of persons of the same sex, March 15th, 2021.

express themselves in the ever-increasing dimension of the divine love.[2]

FS insists in the fact that these blessings are not approving sin. They are all about asking for actual graces for these people to repent and come to the full truth of the Gospel. What about the objection concerning the blessing of two people who are a *couple*? Is the blessing of a couple as such determined by the fact that they come together?

Aquinas' teachings help us to understand that the formal object of the blessing is determined by the words and the intention of the one blessing, not by the people who approach the blessing. The firing squad was blessed by the bishop under the formality he chose with his words and gestures. Similarly, the couple can be blessed and must be blessed only under a certain formality, which the minister freely chooses with his words and intention.

This is the novelty of these *pastoral* blessings. Not that they bless sin, but that they propose, at a magisterial level, Aquinas' teachings on the formal object of *blessings* being coextensive with Christ's *pastoral* charity.

Everything and everyone that Christ's heart loves, can and must be blessed under the same formal aspect in light of which this heart loves. In this way, as God tells us through Saint Paul, "bless and do not curse them" (Rom 12:14).

---

2. *FS*, 31; emphasis added.

Selected Bibliography

Ambrose of Milan. "On the Duties of the Clergy." In *St. Ambrose: Select Works and Letters.* Vol. 10. Translated by H. De Romestin and H. Duckworth. Edited by P. Schaff and H. Wace. A Select Library of the Nicene and Post-Nicene Fathers of the Christian Church, Second Series. Buffalo: Christian Literature, 1896.

Andereggen, Ignacio. *Filosofía Primera: Lecciones aristotélico-dionisiano-tomistas de Metafísica.* Buenos Aires: Dyonisus, 2019.

———. *Fundamentos de la Filosofía Moral de Santo Tomás de Aquino: Lecciones sobre la filosofía y la teología moral de Santo Tomás de Aquino.* Buenos Aires: Dyonisus, 2019.

Aquinas, Thomas. *Catena Aurea in Quatuor Evangelia: Expositio in Matthaeum.* Vol. 1. Edited by A. Guarenti. Taurini-Rome: Marietti, 1953.

———. *Commentary on Aristotle's De Anima.* Translated by Kenelm Foster and Sylvester Humphries. New Haven: Yale University Press, 1951.

———. *Commentary on the Gospel of John.* Translated by F. R. Larcher. Latin/English Edition of the Works of St. Thomas Aquinas 35–36. Green Bay: Aquinas Institute, 2013.

———. *Commentary on the Gospel of Matthew.* Translated by J. Holmes and B. Mortensen. Latin/English Edition of the Works of St. Thomas Aquinas 33–34. Green Bay: Aquinas Institute, 2013.

———. *Commentary on the Letter of Saint Paul to the Galatians.* Translated by F. R. Larcher et al. Edited by J. Mortensen and E. Alarcón. Latin/English Edition of the Works of St. Thomas Aquinas 38. Green Bay: Aquinas Institute, 2012.

———. *Commentary on the Letter of Saint Paul to the Hebrews.* Translated by F. R. Larcher. Edited by J. Mortensen and E. Alarcón. Latin/English Edition of the Works of St. Thomas Aquinas 41. Green Bay: Aquinas Institute, 2012.

———. *Commentary on the Letter of Saint Paul to the Romans.* Translated by F. R. Larcher. Edited by J. Mortensen and E. Alarcón. Latin/English Edition of the Works of St. Thomas Aquinas 37. Green Bay: Aquinas Institute, 2012.

———. *Commentary on the Letters of Saint Paul to the Corinthians.* Translated by F. R. Larcher et al. Edited by J. Mortensen and E. Alarcón. Latin/English Edition of the Works of St. Thomas Aquinas 38. Green Bay: Aquinas Institute, 2012.

———. *Commentary on the Letters of Saint Paul to the Ephesians.* Translated by F. R. Larcher et al. Edited by J. Mortensen and E. Alarcón. Latin/English Edition of the Works of St. Thomas Aquinas 38. Green Bay: Aquinas Institute, 2012.

———. *Commentary on the Letters of Saint Paul to Timothy.* Translated by F. R. Larcher et al. Edited by J. Mortensen and E. Alarcón. Latin/English Edition of the Works of St. Thomas Aquinas 38. Green Bay: Aquinas Institute, 2012.

———. *Disputed Questions on Virtue.* Translated by Jeffrey Hause. Indianapolis: Hackett, 2010.

———. *Expositio Libri Peryermeneias.* Opera omnia iussu Leonis XIII P. M. edita. Vol. 1*/1. Rome-Paris: Commisio Leonina-J. Vrin, 1989.

———. *Expositio super Iob ad litteram.* Opera omnia iussu Leonis XIII P. M. edita. Vol. 26. Rome: Ad Sanctae Sabinae, 1965.

———. *In Psalmos Davidis Expositio. Opera Omnia.* Vol. 14. Parma: Typis Petri Fiaccadori, 1863.

———. *On Evil.* Translated by Richard Regan. Edited by Brian Davies. New York: Oxford University Press, 2003.

———. *Quodlibet I, II, III, VI, IV, V, XII.* Opera omnia jussu Leonis XIII P. M. edita. Vol. 25/1. Rome-Paris: Commissio Leonina-Éditions du Cerf, 1996.

———. *Scriptum Super Libros Sententiarum Magistri Petri Lombardi Episcopi Parisiensis.* Vol 3. Edited by M. F. Moos. Paris: Lethielleux, 1956.

———. *Summa Contra Gentiles.* Edited by John Mortensen and Enrique Alarcon. Translated by Laurence Shapcore. Steubenville: Emmaus Academic, 2019.

———. *Summa Theologiae.* Edited by J. Mortensen and E. Alarcón. Latin/English Edition of the Works of St. Thomas Aquinas 13–20. Green Bay: Aquinas Institute, 2012.

———. *Super Boethium De Trinitate.* Vol 50. Opera Omnia Iussu Leonis XIII. P. M. Edita. Rome: Editori di San Tommaso, 1992.

Augustine of Hippo. *The City of God.* Translated by Marcus Dods. In *St. Augustine's City of God and Christian Doctrine*, edited by Philip Schaff. Buffalo: Christian Literature, 1887.

Bauer Walter, et al. *A Greek-English Lexicon of the New Testament and Other Early Christian Literature.* Chicago: University of Chicago Press, 2000.

Brock, Stephen L. *Action and Conduct: Thomas Aquinas and the Theory of Action.* Washington, DC: Catholic University of America Press, 2021.

———. "Aquinas the Conservationist." In *In Search of Harmony: Metaphysics and Politics*, edited by James G. Hanink. Washington, DC: Catholic University of America Press: 2019.

———. *The Light That Binds: A Study in Thomas Aquinas's Metaphysics of Natural Law.* Eugene, OR: Pickwick, 2020.

————. *The Philosophy of Saint Thomas Aquinas: A Sketch.* Eugene, OR: Wipf & Stock, 2015.

————. "The Specification of Action in St. Thomas: Nonmotivating Conditions in the Object of Intention." *Thomist* 83 (2019) 321–55.

Cassianus, Ioannes, *Collationum XXIV Collectio In Tres Partes Divisa.* In *Patrologia Latina*, vol. 49. Edited by J. P. Migne. Parisiis: excudebat Migne, 1846.

Catechism of the Catholic Church. New York: Doubleday, 1997.

Fabro, Cornelio. *La Nozione Metafisica di Partecipazione secondo S. Tommaso D'Aquino.* Segni: EDIVI, 2005.

Falanga, Anthony Joseph. *Charity: The Form of the Virtues According to Saint Thomas Aquinas.* Washington, DC: Catholic University of America Press, 1948.

Farrell, Walter. *The Fullness of Life: A Companion to the Summa.* Vol. 3. New York: Sheed and Ward, 1940.

Gallagher, Timothy M. *The Discernment of Spirits: An Ignatian Guide for Everyday Living.* New York: Crossroad, 2005.

García López, Jesús. *Metafísica Tomista: Ontología, Gnoseología Y Teología Natural.* Navarra: EUNSA, 2001.

————. *Tomás de Aquino: Maestro Del Orden.* Madrid: Ediciones Pedagógicas, 1996.

George, Marie I. "Aquinas on the Dangers of Natural Virtue and the Control of Natural Vice." *Tópicos* 40 (2011) 13–50.

Jensen, Steven. *Good and Evil Actions: A Journey Through Saint Thomas Aquinas.* Washington, DC: Catholic University of America Press, 2010.

John Paul II. *Man and Woman He Created Them: A Theology of the Body.* Edited by Michael Waldstein. Boston: Pauline Books & Media, 2006.

Levering, Matthew. *The Abuse of Conscience: A Century of Catholic Moral Theology.* Grand Rapids: Eerdmans, 2021.

Mathews, Joshua G. "Blessing." In *Lexham Theological Wordbook.* Edited by Douglas Mangum et al. Lexham Bible Reference Series. Bellingham, WA: Lexham, 2014.

Millán-Puelles, Antonio. *El Interés Por La Verdad.* Madrid: Ediciones Rialp, 1997.

————. *La Libre Afirmación de Nuestro Ser: Una Fundamentación de La ética Realista.* Madrid: Ediciones Rialp, 1994.

Perez-Lopez, Angel. *The Priest as a Man of Justice.* Charlotte: TAN, 2016.

————. *Procreation and the Spousal Meaning of the Body: A Thomistic Argument Grounded in Vatican II.* Eugene, OR: Pickwick, 2017.

————. "Thomas Aquinas: Master of Human Priestly Formation." *Thomist* 88 (2024) 236–43.

Perez-Lopez, Israel, "Educación y relativismo: Un enfoque crítico" *Scripta Fulgentina* 26 (2016) 133–56.

————. *Enseñar a amar educando en la virtud: La perspectiva teleológica de la formación de la personalidad humana en el pensamiento de Antonio Millán-Puelles.* Beau Bassin: Editorial Académica Española, 2018.

————. *La teoría de la conciencia de Antonio Millán-Puelles y Karol Wojtyla: Un estudio comparativo.* Roma: EDUSC, 2017.

Perez-Lopez, Angel, and Israel Perez-Lopez. "Catholic Conscience and Civil Disobedience: The Primacy of Truth." *Nova et Vetera* 20 (2022) 773–92.

Ramírez, Jacobus. *De Caritate: In II-II Summae Theologiae Divi Thomae Expositio (QQ. XXIII-XLIV),* vol. 12, Opera Omnia. Salamanca: San Esteban, 1998.

————. *La Prudencia.* Madrid: Biblioteca Palabra, 1981.

Rhonheimer, Martin. "Benedict XVI's 'Hermeneutic of Reform' and Religious Freedom." *Nova et Vetera* 9 (2011) 1029–54.

————. *Natural Law and Practical Reason: A Thomist View of Moral Autonomy.* Translated by Gerald Malsbary. New York: Fordham University Press, 2000.

————. *The Perspective of Morality: Philosophical Foundations of Thomistic Virtue Ethics.* Translated by Gerald Malsbary. Washington, DC: Catholic University of America Press, 2011.

Rodríguez Luño, Ángel. *Ética General.* Pamplona: EUNSA, 2001.

Rodríguez Luño, Ángel, and Enrique Colom. *Chosen in Christ to Be Saints: Fundamental Moral Theology.* Scotts Valley, CA: CreateSpace Independent, 2014.

Royo Marín, Antonio. *Teología de la Caridad.* Madrid: BAC, 1960.

————. *Teología Moral Para Seglares: Moral Fundamental.* 2 vols. Madrid: BAC, 1986.

————. *Theology of Christian Perfection.* Translated by Jordan Aumann. Eugene, OR: Wipf & Stock, 2012.

Te Velde, Rudi A. *Participation and Substantiality in Thomas Aquinas.* Leiden: Brill, 1995.

Torrell, Jean Pierre. *Christ and Spirituality in St. Thomas Aquinas.* Translated by Bernhard Blankenhorn. Washington, DC: Catholic University of America Press, 2011.

Turonensis, Gregorius. *Vitae Patrum.* In *Patrologia Latina,* vol. 71. Edited by J. P. Migne. Parisiis: excudebat Migne, 1849.

Westberg, Daniel. *Right Practical Reason: Aristotle, Action, and Prudence in Aquinas.* Oxford: Clarendon, 1994.

Wojtyła, Karol. *Sources of Renewal: The Implementation of the Second Vatican Council.* Translated by P. S. Falla. San Francisco: Harper & Row, 1980.

9 798385 227440